SHATTERED LIES

Pamela McClanahan

Developmental Editor, Cynthia Cutts

Library of Congress Control Number: 2017902713
CreateSpace Independent Publishing Platform
North Charleston, South Carolina

ISBN-13: 9781542878104

ISBN-10: 1542878101

Printed in the United States of America

ACKNOWLEDGEMENTS AND DISCLAIMERS

Ahead of anyone or anything else I must give credit to my heavenly Father for this story. There have been many friends and loved ones who have encouraged me along the way, but I wouldn't have a story worth telling if not for our God.

You'll read about many of the people who have blessed me throughout this journey not the least of which is my faithful husband #4, Michael. He is my rock and I love the life I have with him.

Heartfelt thanks go to my "readers" - Jill, Michael and Greg - who invested their valuable time to proofread my story and offer their feedback. I am so grateful.

Another essential person to the completion of this book is my developmental editor, Cynthia Cutts. I had been working on bits and pieces of my story for the last 15 years. After retiring in May of 2015, I became more focused and continued the writing process, but by August of 2016, I knew I couldn't finish this book on my own. Two women I respect greatly had used Cindy's services to write their stories and so I sought her out.

I am so glad I did. Her skill and expertise kept me focused and on a schedule. She picked me up when I would've fallen into the pit of depression reliving parts of my past and she celebrated with me the victory in getting to completion. I am eternally grateful for her support.

From the time I first engaged Cindy, we worked diligently to tell my story in such a way as to cause no harm to anyone else. I have changed names and omitted plenty of details because first, they aren't essential to the point of my story and second, those details are part of other people's stories and are not mine to tell.

As I've worked on this book I've become sensitive to the realization that others in my past may remember details in a different way. All I can say is I have tried to be as accurate as possible; I know this is simply my perspective. While I've told my story as authentically as I can, I would never want to tarnish or diminish the wonderful memories others have had of some of the people in my life. It's just my story.

We ALL have a story. So much of our lives are left untold. It would be my hope that this book may inspire others to tell their stories. Perhaps if we all shared our stories we would understand a bigger picture of the tapestry God is weaving through all our lives.

For all the others in my life...past, present and for the future generations, my sincere desire in writing this book is to give hope and encouragement to those who have found themselves in a pit of despair. It is especially for those who've found themselves in this pit over and over and over again. I'm here to tell you, it is never too late to change. You are never too far from the reach of a loving God.

"For I am convinced that neither death nor life, neither angels nor demons, neither the present nor the future, nor any powers…neither height nor depth, nor anything else in all creation will be able to separate us from the love of God that is in Christ Jesus our Lord." Romans 8:38-39

May you be blessed,
Pamela McClanahan

DEDICATION

To Husband # 4 - Michael,

We haven't always seen eye to eye but when it mattered the most, you stepped up to the plate. You chose to be obedient to God, our marriage and our family, rather than give up when most would have rightfully walked away.

In our 32+ years of marriage, you, Michael, have become my confidant, my best friend, my strongest supporter, my provider and my protector. You are the hero of my story and I am forever grateful God gave me not one, not two, not three, but four chances to find you and hang on tight. Words can never adequately express my love and appreciation for you.

Thank you for walking beside me through this tumultuous journey. I love being your wife... your angel girl.

Love,
Pamela

TABLE OF CONTENTS

FORWARD

By Michael McClanahan

Sitting at the desk in Pamela's studio behind our Northern California home, I have to push aside stacks of journals, sketch books, art supplies and a fishbowl to find a spot to write. My wife craves simplicity but can't help being excited about a dozen things at the same time. The studio is bursting with color and texture, fragrant with the smells of art supplies, essential oils and freshly mown grass outside the opened Dutch door. The barn reflects so many of the things I love about my wife; a glorious mix of energy, talent, love and peace.

When I met Pamela, I was attracted to her intelligence and her gregarious, outgoing personality. But I also appreciated her welcoming spirit, and her genuine love for others. I could feel how Pamela always looked for the best in people. There was so much love exuding from her, I knew she would be a great mother and I wanted her as my life partner.

I've been married to Pamela for over three decades. That sounds like a great story, but in the beginning we struggled and our marriage was emotionally dead. We coexisted for the sake of our child. Those were years of emptiness for us, when each of us longed, in our own way, for a closeness and connection that was missing in our lives. It was our willingness to individually explore our inner selves through the Christian faith that brought our marriage back from the dead. It wasn't easy. It was emotionally difficult to keep steering into our own pain. I loved Pamela, but the loneliness was still there in my life.

When Pamela and I made the decision to fight for our marriage together, we didn't do it alone. A trusted counselor helped us look within, to determine what part each of us played in our disconnect. We had to work on the individual self first, before we could work on us, as a couple.

One of my major hurdles was learning to be vulnerable. My father was an Army colonel, who taught me that emotions were weakness. I had to work through this dichotomy to allow myself to be vulnerable in the fight for my marriage. Sharing emotions was dangerous new territory for me, but I stuck with it. I knew that if I could identify my own weaknesses first, I would have much more success in developing a healthy marriage.

Our plan to renew our marriage required us to depend on God, honestly look at ourselves and develop our faith at the same time. We discovered that unless we became emotionally healthier individuals, we couldn't communicate. Pamela and I were both Christians when we met, but we had a lot to learn about a relationship with God. It took effort and energy to explore and delve into the Bible, to grow spiritually and to develop a strong, personal relationship with God.

As we each worked on our own issues, I discovered that the more I came to know Jesus Christ, the more I knew myself. The most critical piece of the revival of our marriage was that the more Pamela and I brought God into our relationship, the more we were intimately connected to each other. I believe that our creator designed us to be in relationship and the most intimate relationship is a marriage that truly reflects the love of God. God's intention is to make us one with each other. And only with God in the center of marriage, can this be fulfilled. Pamela and I developed a triune marriage; Pamela, God and me. It's the three of us and God is in the middle.

No marriage is perfect. It took daily, intentional communication, and a willingness to be vulnerable with each other to put me and Pamela on the right path. In the resurrection of our marriage, we surrendered our lives to each other. Our marriage isn't 50/50 now, our marriage is 100/100 - a complete gift of my life to Pamela and her life to me.

This process was painful, emotional, troubling and definitely not easy. The good news is that God really honored that. As you read *Shattered Lies*, you will see that God honored us in a big way. God brought our marriage back from the dead and he continues to bless it every day.

Shattered Lies is a divinely ordained story of how God is faithful. It's a true account of how a desperate search for intimacy drove a sweet, talented, vivacious woman from the emotional turmoil of broken relationships to a quiet, divine peace and a successful, loving relationship with me.

I survived through Pamela's struggles and her victories. And at last, I have arrived at a place where I thrive. I'm no longer surviving my marriage to Pamela, I'm thriving and it's a beautiful place to be.

INTRODUCTION

I have been keeping journals for more than 40 years. They catalogue some of my most incredible joys and some of my deepest shame and heartache. My writings unfold a journey that began with abandonment and lack of nurturing, which manifested into a life mission - to fiercely guard my heart and to prove my worth by being better than the best.

Shattered Lies is a story filled with selfishness, regret, betrayal, desperation and finally healing and redemption. Looking back on my life has not been easy. In fact it's been painful. I've been riding an emotional roller coaster as I've re-visited how hard I searched for love in all the wrong places, only to accumulate three divorces and numerous stress related illnesses by the time I was 25 years old.

I grew up fast with responsibilities that shouldn't have been mine. I learned early on to be a good care-giver, people-pleaser, hard worker and overall Superwoman. I took on every new obstacle like a challenge…a game for me to beat. I developed a competitive, tenacious spirit and very little stood in my way. On the other side of that coin, I was like a pin-ball being ricocheted from one situation to the next with little or no real control. I was a mess. And I was in denial.

By the time I was 25 I felt like I was 80. How I got there is certainly a big part of this story, but the reason for *Shattered Lies* is what happened next. I was a staunch atheist, having disregarded Christianity because of the so called "believers" I observed behaving in selfish, disrespectful and judgmental ways. And then a dear uncle, whom I respected, came along and told me the truth about Christianity and what it really meant to be a Christian. Since there was virtually nowhere to go but up, I decided to check it out for myself.

It took me quite a few years to understand and fully embrace the life God was offering to me, but once I did I wished I'd done it WAY earlier! Doing life hand-in-hand with the God of the Universe is amazing. He has shown himself to be real and completely faithful through all of my life's circumstances.

For the last 15 years as I wrote in my prayer journals and poured out my heart to God, the two messages I consistently received were, "write your story" and "tell your story." But as I began the task of telling my story, I realized that in reality, *Shattered Lies* is His story. It's a story of how the God of the Universe stepped intimately into my life and made something unbelievably beautiful from my mess.

I am not the only one who has experienced debilitating health crises, failed relationships, estrangement from a loved one, or catastrophic financial ruin. I believe God wants me to share my story as an encouragement to someone who may still be in the worst of times. If that's you, or someone you love, I hope you will be encouraged, because *Shattered Lies* has been written for those who feel hopeless, ashamed, angry and disappointed. My story is not one I'm proud of, but I cannot deny the miraculous work God has done in my life since I surrendered to him. My life is living proof that there is another way, and a much better way than I imagined. If your life is a mess, take comfort. Your story is not finished yet. You too, can shatter your lies.

Blessings,
Pamela

1

DESPERATE AND ALONE

Nervously I jingled my keys and tucked my soft fleece scarf around my neck as I walked down the steps of my front porch. I felt disoriented and my heart ached with so much sadness I thought it might stop beating altogether. After three failed marriages, I had just confessed to my fourth husband that I'd been having an affair. The carnage of my deceit twisted inside me. Mentally I was preparing to pack and move on, but where? I felt completely alone and without hope.

I climbed in my car, and in desperation, I headed out of the city into the Sierra foothills where I knew I would find my pastor. I craved wisdom and direction, but I wasn't sure what to expect from a minister once I told him the truth. This was all my fault. It was always my fault.

I pushed hard on the gas, as the car began the steep grade of the narrow country road. It was cold outside, and the bright yellow California sun hadn't quite melted all the ice on the mountain road. Recklessly, I pushed my Subaru station wagon faster, crossing the center line as I navigated sharp turns, then slamming on my brakes as I slid on a patch of black ice, around to the next turn. My anguish manifested into desperate sobs of guilt and I had a sudden realization why people killed themselves.

The car careened around another sharp turn and I stomped on the accelerator to push the car up the next hill as fast as it would go. My heart was dark, but my mind was filled with glaring, vivid memories of the ugly, guilty failures of my life. A cacophony of panic, regret and despair were colliding in my head and the pieces were falling down around my heart. I needed to end this; I couldn't stand another moment of guilt, shame and remorse.

I kept driving, completely engulfed in my regret, knowing that I had carefully guarded my heart; always calculating how to leave a relationship before I could be abandoned. I worked hard at keeping isolation and hurt at bay. But this time I couldn't just walk away. No matter how much I wanted to end this shame, I was stuck firmly in it, because this time God was in the mix.

"Oh God," I cried out in the car. "It would be so easy to just end it right now." As I approached another sharp turn, I pressed hard on the gas pedal. "I could just fly off the road, and I would be dead." I wanted this pain to be done, over, and no longer mine.

But I kept driving, tears flowing so freely, that I could barely see the curves or the majestic emerald conifers ahead. I kept speeding, then slamming on my brakes just enough to make the sharp turns. My heart twisted inside and I could hardly breathe.

All my life I had craved the feeling of being loved. I yearned to feel safe and accepted. But no matter where I found success, I didn't find love. And now this final crushing blow of a fourth failed marriage and breaking the heart of a good man, was more than my pain threshold could bear. Darkness shrouded me, depression hovered over me and I knew that I couldn't fake this happy, loving, confident, successful persona anymore. I wanted to disappear.

I had suffered major failures before. But this time the damage to my soul was too deep to go on. My sorrowful heart wrenched in agony. I pulled into the church parking lot and shut off the engine. In the quiet of the car interior, I grabbed a tissue and mopped up my tears. I flipped down the visor and looked at the broken soul that stared at me from the mirror. How the hell did I get here?

2

GROWING PAINS

When I was a little girl, my mother used to call me Pamela Gail Farcy Darcy. It's a goofy name but it totally fits the little girl who still lives inside me. She was full of life. She loved to dance and sing and do cartwheels everywhere she went. She made people smile! She was sunshine; full of life and hope and expectation.

In her early years, Pamela Gail Farcy Darcy believed in fairy tales, Prince Charming and happily ever after. Pamela believed that families stayed together and she looked forward to the day when her Prince Charming would sweep her off her feet, marry her and treasure her forever.

Unlike the innocent little girl I wanted to be, my life was tainted with adults who abandoned or betrayed me, oblivious to the damage they were inflicting and forced me to become an adult long before I was ready. My dreams were shattered and cruel realities replaced my expectations.

The memories I have of my mom are a mixed bag of raw emotion. As I was growing up, Mom reminded me a lot of Lucille Ball. In fact *I love Lucy* was one of mom's favorite shows.

I think she probably got some of her wilder trickster ideas from watching Lucy's character fall from one predicament to another. Mom had a devilish side when it came to playing tricks on people. The sneakier, more shocking and embarrassing the better! I remember a time when some neighbors went out of town and asked mom to watch over their house. Weary from a long drive and a full week of activities, they came home late at night to find all the lightbulbs removed from every lamp in their house, their beds short-sheeted and all of their undergarments frozen solid. Mom thought it was hilarious.

On another occasion, when Dad was getting ready to leave on a long business trip, she packed a magazine in the bottom of his suitcase. Dad was traveling with his boss and sharing a room. As Dad unpacked his suitcase he found a Playboy magazine. His boss picked it up and casually started thumbing through the magazine only to find Mom's face taped in various sizes and expressions over the bodies of the women throughout the magazine. Dad had no idea what she had done.

At the same time, mom was a really big giver. If anyone needed anything, all they had to do was call mom and she would move heaven and earth to make it happen. Mom gave way beyond her means using credit whenever necessary to show someone she was thinking of them. Mom was welcoming. She loved meeting new people and built many loyal friendships. She never forgot a birthday or anniversary and always reached out with phone calls or letters. Sometimes it felt like she spent more time caring about near strangers than her own family. Perhaps that was her comfort zone.

Mom volunteered at my school for anything that required creativity and craftsmanship. She always said yes when asked to make posters for everything from student government to upcoming events. She enjoyed creating costumes for special holidays and loved dressing up along with the kids.

Every Christmas I looked forward to a new hand-made flannel nightgown from Mom. I loved those nightgowns. They were soft and comforting. Over the years Mom sewed with love one embroidered square after another until she'd made personalized quilts for each of her grandchildren. And on your birthday you were guaranteed to have a special cake designed just for you. Mom was widely known for her custom birthday cakes.

On the cooking front, Mom got by. One of my favorite treats was the Pineapple Upside Down Cake she made in the cast iron skillet on the stove. She could pull together a fantastic dinner, minus the murdered vegetables, when Dad was at home or company was coming. Otherwise she specialized in Banquet TV dinners or Campbell's soup with a hot dog or grilled Velveeta cheese sandwich. It wasn't fancy but we never went without.

Mom had a zest for life that was bigger than her ability to obtain it. She hinted relentlessly until others offered to take her places and when they did, she enjoyed herself to the fullest. She left a positive, full-of-life impression everywhere she went. I have yet to encounter anyone who met her that doesn't have a fond or happy memory of my mom.

But behind closed doors it was a different story. To the outside world I believe mom projected the life she wanted to have. But once inside, it was as if she didn't have the confidence to believe any of it and she withdrew into depression and violent mood swings. She was a different person.

Mom was a narcissist. She maintained strict control over her environment and grew angry when she didn't get her way. At the same time, she was a victim. Seemingly incapable of functioning, she demanded the attention of her family. And most of the time that meant me.

My mom was an emotional wreck. She was needy, volatile and slipped easily into the victim role, clinging to me like a drowning victim threatening to take me down with her if I tried to let go. Mom had to be the center of attention all the time. I learned early to fade into the wallpaper to avoid conflict with Mom. In the privacy of our home, she was always unhappy and it was always someone else's fault.

My sister, Kathy, three years older than I, was physically abused by Mom and neglected by Dad, which left her completely vulnerable to all sorts of trouble. Kathy's world with Mom was evil and violent and as a result, Kathy was constantly surrounded by negative messages about her worth as a person.. It was common for Mom to scream and hurl items against the wall in her fury, with Kathy hunkered down, hiding in the midst of broken pieces.

My sister grew up feeling unwanted by both of our parents. The only time she recalls feeling safe was when she got to visit the neighbors, who lovingly asked her to call them, Nana and Papa. During one such visit, Nana was rocking three year old Kathy, holding her close and speaking sweetly over the child who appeared to be sleeping. Nana commented on what a peaceful little angel Kathy was and Mom harshly replied, "That girl has never been anything but trouble since the day she was born. I give her a spanking every day whether she needs it or not." With her eyes closed, Kathy's body tensed as she felt Nana squeeze her just a little closer. She really didn't understand why her mama hated her.

Around the same time, Kathy recalls Mom bursting into her dark bedroom with a handful of metal bobby pins from the bathroom. Kathy had just taken a bath and was already in bed and sleeping. Abruptly turning on the overhead light, Mom glared at Kathy as she warned, "Don't EVER put these into an electrical outlet." She repeated the admonition, pointing to an electric socket, then left the bobby pins on Kathy's bedside table. As soon as Mom left, a precocious and curious Kathy got out of bed and stuck a bobby pin into the outlet. An electric shock rocked Kathy three feet back onto the floor. Even as a toddler, Kathy wondered if her mother was trying to kill her.

This was the recurring theme of my sister's life in our home. Like me, Kathy has vivid memories of Mom and Dad fighting and screaming nearly every night they were together. After many of these fights Mom would drive the knife a little deeper telling both Dad and Kathy that, "Everything was fine until SHE came along."

It wasn't until high school when Kathy's English teacher asked about a brutal black eye, that Kathy told anyone about the violence our mother displayed behind closed doors. Out of the blue one day, Kathy and I were both picked up by a police officer and taken to the Children's Receiving Home 'for our safety.' However, when authorities looked into the reported abuse, Mom spun a conniving and manipulative story that put Kathy and me back into our home one week later. No one ever explained anything to us and of course, nothing changed.

Even when Kathy ran away from home at 15, my parents didn't report her missing; and when Kathy finally returned home after a week of absence, she found no comfort or concern - only the cruel announcement that our parents had given away her beloved dog Kilo. They had taken her puppy to the pound.

"We thought you weren't coming back," Mom told her matter-of-factly. That was the final crushing blow. Kathy resigned herself to give up any hope of ever being loved in our house.

Dad was never physically abusive to Kathy but he didn't protect her either. The only time Kathy ever felt loved by Dad was when he was drunk. In those times he would get very sentimental and hold her close, telling her he loved her and was sorry.

My memories of Dad are peppered with his absence. Dad left our home often, sometimes to go to a bar; other times to go out of town for work. I coveted the time I had with Dad, and if he was home, I just wanted to be with him. I went with him as he ran errands, or just down to the local gas station to fill up the three tanks he had on the pickup. Every year we could count on being with Dad at least three times: first to go camping for a week at Anchor Bay on California's north coast; second to go deer hunting for a week at a camp near Sterling City, CA and third, when Dad took me and Kathy to the Christmas tree lot down the street to choose our tree together. He was typically quiet and I loved his Texan ways, his southern drawl and how he sang along with country music songs like "Don't Fence Me In." We enjoyed playing chess or just hanging out, him telling his corny jokes and flashing his beautiful smile. When Dad was at home we had fun together, but all these memories are laced with sadness, because I knew he would soon be gone again.

When Dad was home, he and Mom were always in conflict. I remember telling someone once that My mom and dad screamed and fought every night for 10 straight years. As an adult I know that wasn't possible because Dad wasn't ever home for 10 straight years, but the intensity of the unrest felt that heavy. Mom yelled and whined and blamed Dad for everything she saw wrong in her life. Prone to temper tantrums, she'd often start screaming and throwing things. Dad drank to numb the stress of Mom's relentless nagging. Kathy took off to find refuge amongst her friends and I hid in my room turning up my record player to drown out the fighting, finding comfort with James Taylor and Carole King. As much as I wanted to believe that families laughed and loved together, my reality was a completely dysfunctional family, fraught with anger and conflict. We were not a family at all; just four individuals living in the same house, each trying to survive.

3

TURNING POINT

D espite living in my reality, I still strove to be that happy, little butterfly who wanted to be the best at everything, in the hope that I could be loved and valued. I poured myself into school and gymnastics and developed into a strong performer. I loved receiving praise and recognition when I did well. I loved the days when Dad came home from his business trips, and we could play chess together or he'd let me "help" him work on the car or truck in the driveway.

One warm August day when I was 14, Dad came home from a TDY job he had been working in Florida for the previous nine months. Dad was a Civil service contractor who worked with the military to inspect the integrity of welded seams on aircraft. When a plane went down somewhere in the world, he was called in to inspect what went wrong and then raise the flag for the inspection of other planes of the same variety to make sure those same vulnerabilities weren't widespread among the fleet. He told me TDY stood for Temporary Duty Yonder... I had missed him so much I couldn't say YES fast enough when he asked me to go for a ride with him in his pickup. Excited for some time alone, I jumped in the cab and he drove us to Carmichael Park.

Dad pulled the truck over next to a curb in the park. I loved it there. Even on the hottest Sacramento days the dozens of mature oaks and majestic maples provided a cool shady retreat. But instead of spreading a well-worn quilt for a father-daughter picnic, we stayed in the pickup and I learned that dad was going to divorce Mom. Dad confessed that he had fallen in love with another woman. Her name was Nora and he had been living with her in Florida for the previous nine months. Dad went on to explain that he had brought Nora back with him to California, and had moved her into an apartment nearby. He wanted me to meet her. Dad continued to map out the new life he planned without mom, telling me that he planned to marry Nora as soon as the divorce from Mom was final. And he did exactly as he planned. The very day after Mom and Dad's divorce was final, Dad married Nora in a cheesy chapel in Reno.

I believe that day in the cab of my father's truck at Carmichael Park was the last official day of my childhood. It was definitely a turning point.

It had always been hard for Mom with Dad working out of town so much. But now, after a painful blur of 18 months of court appearances and irreconcilable differences, she was divorced and she collapsed into a total wreck. After 26 years of marriage her world was rocked. My sister Kathy was 18. She couldn't stand Mom's irrational and selfish behavior, so Kathy moved in with her boyfriend, who turned out to be an abuser. When Kathy came home two weeks later, instead of finding mom with open arms, she found Mom holding a garage sale of all Kathy's belongings. Defeated, Kathy went back to that abusive relationship and lived in fear for the next seven years.

From my perspective, Mom drove my dad and sister away. I blamed her for Dad's drinking and for badgering him so much he finally couldn't take it anymore. As Dad was moving out, I vividly recall an argument they had. Mom had run after Dad out to the garage in a violent rage. Her tirade escalated as he didn't respond to her wild threats. But finally, she pushed the right buttons, and the fight was on. I was standing near Dad, right next to his work bench, and yet I must have been invisible as their angry, bitter words darted around my head.

Dad picked up a turquoise portable radio Mom had given him for a birthday present. It was what we always listened to when he was working on one of the cars. Mom insisted that it was hers, and told Dad he couldn't take it. They verbally bantered the topic around until Dad finally put the radio down and said, "Keep it. I just won't send you any child support or alimony."

In that instant, I knew that if Mom and I were going to survive without Dad, I had to be in charge. Dad was obviously leaving and he offered no invitation for me to go with him. My world had shrunk, everybody else was gone, and somehow in my adolescent brain I knew that I was on my own now. My childhood was all locked up and it was my responsibility to take care of Mom. It didn't appear there were any other options.

I resigned myself to finish high school quickly and become the family leader. Stuffing pain away, I felt sad that I didn't have a mother who could take care of me or someone that I could go to with my feelings of grief and abandonment.

Dad left that day and Mom and I stayed in our home, unconsciously trading roles.

For years I judged my mother harshly, thinking if she had not been so immature and self-centered she would have been more loving and less demanding, which could have prevented the divorce. Later I learned that Mom had been orphaned at 14 and sent to live with whoever would take her in. No doubt that was a turning point in her life, too; one that stopped her from growing up emotionally. I can't imagine what her life must have been like. Even though I judged her bitterly for many years I now try to think of Mom with empathy and appreciation for the strong qualities she developed against all odds.

I was only 14, but I obtained a work permit and took a 30 hour a week job during my first year of high school as a telephone solicitor, and I became the breadwinner in our household. Each day after school, I sat at a narrow table facing a blank wall in a hotel conference room with a telephone and a dot matrix computer printout of prospects. I made cold call after cold call selling, "$250 worth of valuable goods and services," for only $13.95! It was a heck of a deal and I was pretty good at it.

By 17, I realized I could live on my own, enjoying independence and my own apartment, where I wouldn't have to take care of Mom. So I gave Mom an ultimatum. With little emotion I boldly told her, "Mom, either get a job or I'm moving out."

Lo and behold, she did just that. With two incomes our budget improved and we made a plan to finish paying off the house. I grew up quickly and learned how to be productive and efficient. I took summer classes and zero period so I could graduate from high school a year early. I was becoming Super-woman - on the outside. Inside, I was still a little girl wanting to sit on her daddy's lap. But there was no time for that anymore.

4

SEARCHING FOR MY PRINCE

Besides the telephone solicitor job, I worked as a busser and dishwasher at a local convalescent home, which is where I met my first husband. He was beautiful, with thick blond locks, a big, warm smile and the physique of a water polo player. He was kind and funny and so many other things. We went steady all through high school.

At 18, we were married and six months later I walked out. Over the next seven years I married and divorced twice more. Remember that Cinderella story? I just couldn't give up.

In my first marriage, after careful review and the benefit of hindsight, I can see that my desperate need for love and my ever-present fear of abandonment set me up to leave first before I could get hurt. The complete truth is, I met someone, while studying at the college library, who showed me a bigger world of nature and adventure that was mine for the taking. I was seduced by the possibilities.

I tried talking to H#1 about these new revelations but he was laser-focused on the fast track to accomplishing our predefined goals. This "talk" of mine would just take us off course and delay our plans.

Impulsively I walked out just six months after marrying the man I'd been in love with for the previous four years. I was selfish, stubborn and too immature to listen to anyone. H#1 tried repeatedly to get me to reconsider. He even offered to buy a motorcycle and take me across Canada. I think he would have done just about anything. I never looked back.

Ironically, my first husband was undoubtedly the most loving, kind, considerate and unpretentious man I had ever met up to that time. He loved me unconditionally and I felt it. He was even with me when, at 15, I had a benign breast tumor that had to be surgically removed. I'd grown up with a really low self-image being flat-chested, tall and skinny. Mom loved to say, "If she turns sideways and sticks out her tongue she looks just like a zipper." But this man just loved me. For decades after I walked out I yearned for a relationship where I felt "good enough."

Newly divorced at 19 years of age, I hooked up with my new-found adventurous, motorcycle riding, mountain man. We were together for four tumultuous years. Initially we had a lot of fun, riding his Triumph motorcycle to places like Yosemite, traveling light and experiencing life to the fullest.

We both worked at McCurry Camera Stores and both attended California State University, Sacramento. It was dreamy, until we had to pay bills or repair the car or face any other adult responsibilities. We lived full and hard, using our share of drugs and alcohol. After all, it was the 70's in California.

One of the very best parts of this relationship was our son. I became pregnant in April, 1978 and after completing that semester, we moved to San Diego where H#2 began work on his Master's Degree. I took the summer off school and worked in an exotic pet store. I have always loved most every kind of creature and I regularly brought home parrots or rare finches that needed some extra care.

When we first arrived in San Diego we were drawn to a place called Ocean Beach. It sounded PERFECT. What we didn't realize was that it was directly below the flight pattern of incoming flights to San Diego International Airport. We didn't stay very long because I was convinced the reverberations from the planes overhead were causing a tsunami effect with my amniotic fluid. That couldn't be good for the baby.

We found a beautiful flat in an older home just above downtown San Diego. By offering to pay a hefty pet deposit, I convinced the landlord to let us move in with Apollo, our enormous (half-human) Irish Setter, and an aviary full of birds.

On February 10, 1979, on the pull-down Murphy bed in our living room, I gave birth to a beautiful nine pound baby boy. It was amazing.

I remember being absolutely elated when I first found out I was pregnant. I laid down on the bed with my hands gently cradling my abdomen, knowing there was a precious life growing inside of me. I loved this child before I ever knew him.

We had planned to give birth at Kaiser until we went to a birthing class where we were completely turned off. It had a cold, sterile, mass production type atmosphere and we wanted more. The very next day I called all over San Diego until I was put in touch with a beautiful, gentle and very knowledgeable midwife named Diane Smith.

I studied everything I could get my hands on to become prepared for childbirth. We wanted to create a safe, healthy and loving atmosphere for our child to enter the world...and that we did.

In addition to our midwife, Diane, we had a registered nurse, a professional photographer (recommended by Diane), my sister and H#2's mom. It was a celebration I could not have imagined. The photographer did a beautiful job capturing the palpable love and awe that was present in our San Diego living room that day. I will always treasure those images and memories.

Almost instantly after giving birth, my heart was forever changed. The child I had been imagining for the last nine months was now cradled in my arms, surrounded by loved ones. Spiritually, I was hovering somewhere between atheism and agnosticism, yet deep in my soul I knew this was a miracle. In a matter of moments the weight of the world fell on my shoulders and I knew I would do everything I could to love and protect this child.

We named him Jesse.

I hadn't spoken to my dad in the nearly seven years since he divorced Mom but suddenly I knew I had to call him. I wanted him to know he had a grandson. It was the start of a beautiful reconciliation.

For the upcoming summer, H#2 obtained a fantastic seasonal job as a Park Ranger at Lassen Volcanic National Park. We moved into park housing in the tiny town of Mineral, California, with our three month old son. It seemed as if I had been plopped right in the middle of a fairy tale. The mountain air was fresh and the pace was peaceful. Everything seemed right.

As Fall approached, I tutored children in the town's only one-room school, bringing Jesse with me...bundled up in a hooded wicker basket. H#2 picked up substitute teaching jobs in nearby Red Bluff but winter was coming and the road would soon become as difficult to manage as our mountain of debt. It only took a few short months after that extraordinary summer ended to realize it was impossible to make ends meet. Defeated, we moved back to Sacramento, staying briefly with my dad and stepmom while we looked for an affordable house to rent. We ended up on 57th Street just east of downtown Sacramento.

As in many fairy tales, things change. I wanted our perfect family to be happy and forever, but as months passed it became clear that wasn't going to happen. Plagued by my past and worried about my future, I felt that I had no choice, but to take my son and leave H#2.

I began to carve out my new life, boldly preparing to face the challenges of being a single mom. But nothing could have prepared me for the shock of a court decision to award full custody of my precious child to H#2. Out of respect for my ex-husband and the positive relationship we've built over the last 35 years I won't go into the details that ended our marriage. You need only know that we both fiercely loved Jesse and the decision to leave was not made lightly.

Eventually H#2 and I developed an amicable relationship and we settled into a pattern of joint custody. H#2 was always a devoted father, but ultimately he also became my trusted friend. I am happy that he found a wonderful woman to marry. She is, at once, both tough and soft, sassy and sweet, loving and hilarious. If I had to share the job of mothering with anyone, I'm glad it was with this kind-hearted woman.

Then along came a spider...

H#3 was tall, dark and handsome with perfect dimples and a well-practiced smile that drew you in. Eleven years my senior, he was a professional photographer and he saw something in me. He bought me new clothes and had my hair and make-up done. He was creating in me the 'something' he had seen. In hindsight, what he wanted was a Barbie doll, with a dark side.

I was so torn. Desperately motivated to create a picture perfect family environment where I could proudly and comfortably have Jesse part time, I married H#3 even though I'm sure if I had known how to listen to the truth deep inside of me, I would have walked away.

H#3 was a narcissist, with a capital N. Everything had to be perfect, including me, all the time. This was the darkest and most shame-filled of all my relationships. I still can't talk about the details but suffice it to say there came a day when a line was crossed that I would no longer step over with him. I'd had enough. I went to work the next day and asked a dear friend if he would follow me home in his pickup and go in with me while I grabbed a few things. It was unnervingly tense but I got out of there.

Three divorces; I was going on 25 and I felt like a pile of filthy rags. I couldn't escape the shame. It was becoming clear to me that life sucked. I was bitter and resentful.

After leaving H#3, I got a place of my own in midtown Sacramento. It was the first time in my life I had ever lived alone, and I loved it. I rented the bottom right flat in a 1920's four-plex with lots of built-ins and swaths of natural light. There was a huge porch on the front of the house where I sat in my rocking chair watching my yellow parakeet swinging in a cage that hung on a nearby stand.

Though I tried to create a peaceful, happy existence, everything I did seemed hard. I'd been working full time and going to college part time for nearly seven years and the end was nowhere in sight. I was passed over at work for a promotion to outside sales and I just couldn't seem to catch a break. I was in the midst of a painful custody battle over my son and I didn't think things could get much worse.

One cool, winter evening, as I meandered through art galleries in the heart of midtown, I met a guy named David. We were admiring the same piece of art when we looked up and caught each other's gaze. We struck up an easy conversation as we continued to wander the nearby studios. I learned that he lived in the neighborhood and over the next few weeks we spent a fair amount of time together.

One night, we went to Safeway to pick up something for dinner. As we were looking for the "best" check-out lane I made a comment that, "With my luck, whatever lane we pick will end up being the longest." David didn't say much until he drove me home later that evening. Instead of coming inside, as he usually did, he walked me up the freshly painted concrete steps onto the porch and stopped outside my door. Calmly, he held my hands in both of his and said, "I won't be seeing you anymore." With an expression of shock and confusion I asked him why.

David dropped my hand. He looked off to the street light and rubbed the back of his neck. "Pamela," he turned back to look at me. "Ever since I've met you, I've seen a recurring pattern of behavior. In almost every situation, you think of yourself as a victim... 'You'll always find the longest line'."

I backed up a step and pulled my sweater up around my shoulders, shaking my head.

But David went on. "What you think and what you say, whether aloud or to yourself, can profoundly impact your life.

I believe that you can choose not to be the victim all the time. But I can't invest anymore time or energy in this relationship waiting to find out if you will."

"But David," I started to argue.

"I hope you have a good life, Pamela," David continued. "I wish you well, but this is it for me. Good bye." He turned and walked away.

As I closed the front door my shock quickly transformed into rage. I was boiling inside. VICTIM? I beg your pardon! My mom was a victim and I will never be like my mom! He might as well have slapped me hard across the face. The sting was palpable.

After a while, with a glass of red wine, I started thinking about what David had said. His words kept rolling around in my head. I thought about the comment I made in the grocery store and wondered if David could be right. Can the messages we surround ourselves with become self-fulfilling prophecies? I pondered the idea.

Over the next weeks I became very interested in self-help. I read books about positive thinking and listened to cassette tapes by psychologists like Dr. Wayne Dyer. I even went back to my employer, Gary, and asked him why I was passed over for the outside sales job. With a kind, almost fatherly manner, he told me that I had some "growing up" to do. He encouraged me to continue my pursuit of self-growth and also suggested I take a Dale Carnegie Course in Effective Speaking and Human Relations. He believed it could help me in the area of confidence. I did just that.

5

NOWHERE ELSE TO GO

Near the end of my relationship with H#3, I learned my dad was diagnosed with esophageal cancer. Dad had been married to Nora for about 8 years now, and we had just been reconciled a short time since Jesse's birth. I still loved my dad dearly and I was heartbroken to think that he could die.

I'll never forget the day. I was at the Kaiser Hospice Center on Cottage Way in Sacramento, hoping for a time when Dad's room would empty of visitors so I could go and make my peace with him. The waiting room was completely empty. Not just of people - it felt devoid of everything. Or maybe it was just me who couldn't feel anything.

My dear Uncle Jim found me sitting there alone, buckling under the weight of the world; all of my failures stacked squarely upon my shoulders. He sat down next to me, put his hand on my knee and said, "I think I know what you need. Come with me." And so I did. As we walked out to his pickup in the parking lot I thought he was going to take me for something to eat or drink. Instead, we just sat in the cab.

He looked at me with love and compassion in his face and reached for my hand. "Pamela," he said, with his left arm resting on the top of the steering wheel, "I've watched you fight through life and get into some pretty bad messes."

"I know, I've made a lot of mistakes," I admitted to him.

"Well they weren't all your fault," Uncle Jim said, "I just hate to see you suffer so much. I think I know what you need..."

I braced myself, thinking there was a lecture coming, never taking my eyes off of his.

But he smiled a soft smile and said, "Pamela, I think you need Jesus in your life."

"Ha!" I thought to myself. God wasn't in our house when I was a little girl. There were no sweet bedtime stories about how much Jesus loved me. Periodically I joined my neighbor to attend Sunday school and I have pictures of my sister and me kneeling for bedtime prayers, but I don't remember any emphasis or understanding of God in our household. The only time we went to church was on Easter or Christmas when we would dress up in fancy clothes, usually with our cousins, aunts and uncles. Then we put God back in his box until the next major holiday came around. I really didn't know anything about God. In fact, most of the Christians I knew were rather annoying. When Dad introduced me to Nora, he told me she was a "good Christian woman," but I wasn't impressed. She stole my father from me, and she acted stuck-up and "holier than thou." She didn't care about me or offer to help me in any way.

It had been easy to push God out of my life and remain disconnected from him. I knew very little of what the Bible actually said. What I observed, was mostly a lot of people who called themselves Christians and behaved in selfish, unfriendly, disrespectful and judgmental ways. I had disregarded Christianity long ago and decided I could do better on my own. I didn't know what to say to this. I loved and respected my uncle.

With my Dad dying across the parking lot, there didn't seem anywhere else to turn. I thought, "Why not? Nothing else is working."

Looking out the pickup window I sighed, "Well, you are right," I swallowed a big lump in my throat. "I'm not doing very well on my own. I guess it can't hurt to check it out."

And then, right there in that old pickup truck, Uncle Jim walked me through a few passages in the Bible, and he led me through a prayer, asking Jesus into my life.

I remember he started with John 3:16 , "For God so loved the world that he gave his one and only son that whoever believes in him shall not perish but have eternal life." I knew my dad had accepted Christ into his life and it seemed this was saying that if I did that too, I could one day be reunited with my real dad as well as a heavenly father. That sounded too good to be true.

Uncle Jim went on to share verses from Paul's letter to the Romans. He told me, "For all have sinned and fall short of the Glory of God." Romans 3:23 And then he read from Romans 6:23, "For the wages of sin is death, but the gift of God is eternal life in Christ Jesus our Lord."

I was relieved to hear that "everyone sins and falls short," because it seemed that no one could have screwed up as much as me. I found a glimmer of hope in these words.

After sharing a few more verses, we joined hands. Uncle Jim told me to repeat after him, "Heavenly Father, You know I've made a lot of mistakes. My life is pretty messed up. Please forgive me and save me. I need Jesus to be my Savior. Please take over my life. Amen."

When it was over, there wasn't an immediate parting of the clouds with a dove descending or anything like that, but I did feel a connection to something. I hoped it was God. I was cynical and skeptical but I basically said, "OK God, if you're real, I need you to show up."

Then I hugged my uncle and got out the truck. I knew Dad's days on earth were limited and I desperately wanted some one-on-one time with him, but his room was always full of people.

I walked back inside the Hospice Center, lost and forlorn. It had been less than two years after reconciling with my dad, and now he was dying from cancer. He had been a pretty heavy smoker most of his life and apparently it had caught up with him. I was devastated and there was so much I wanted to tell him.

To have lost him once when I was 14 was tragic, but to be on the verge of losing him again at 25 was unbearable. I was completely spent. Empty. It felt like I was holding on to the last knot at the bottom of a thick rope suspended over the Grand Canyon and I didn't have the strength to hang on. I sat down on a chair against the wall outside Dad's room, and drawing my feet up onto the edge of the seat, I rested my head on my knees, and quietly let the tears fall.

Then someone sat down next to me. I assumed it was a nurse but now I believe it was an angel. "Are you okay?" the angel asked, gently rubbing my shoulder.

"My dad is dying and I just want some private time with him," I sobbed. I rarely cried, but I was desperate to have my father to myself. I brushed my tears away and took a deep breath. "His room is jammed with visitors and it's impossible to have a private conversation with him."

"Oh sweetheart," She gently hugged me, "Just come back tonight, after 10 p.m. when visiting hours are over. Your dad will still be awake and no one will interrupt you then."

Pamela, the rule-follower, would never have considered violating any visiting hour rules, but I decided that if a nurse gave me permission, it would be okay.

I went back that night, just past 10 p.m. and gathered my courage for a few more minutes before walking in the front door, past the reception desk and into Dad's room. He smiled when he saw me. I sat on the bed and held his hand. Looking deeply into those beautiful brown eyes, I told him about Michael, who I had just started dating and I remember seeing the sadness settle across his face.

"Honey, I just want you to be happy," Dad said. "That's all that matters to me."

It felt good to know that Dad wanted me to be happy. I had loved him so much as a child. When he left us to marry Nora, I felt abandoned and betrayed. It hurt to think that I had been mad at him for seven years and now that we were reconciling, he was dying.

"Thank you for working so hard for our family," I told Dad, remembering all the things I treasured about him. "I remember you working, sometimes three different jobs at a time, to provide for us. And even with your busy work schedule you still managed to take the 'new math' classes, so you could help me with my homework."

Dad grinned at that memory. I continued, "Thank you for teaching me how to play chess. I love how you challenged me intellectually. I will always remember the many games we played on that ornate black and gold set you brought me from Thailand. Oh Dad, I love you so much."

The tears started to flow and as his arms reached for me, I laid down beside him on his bed. Though his 6 foot 4 inch frame was weak and thin, having been ravaged by cancer, he held me close and I felt safe. We cried together and I snuggled beneath his protective wing. He told me he was sorry for how things had turned out. He was sorry I had struggled so hard for so long. His acknowledgment meant the world to me.

"Did you know that I accepted Jesus?" I asked Dad. I knew that Dad had become a born-again believer of Jesus since meeting Nora.

"Oh honey, that's the best news ever," he said through tears and a big smile. "I want you to read Psalm 23. It's my favorite."

I had a chance to introduce Dad to Michael not long before he died at the age of 54. A year and a half later, when I was 26, I married Michael. A fourth marriage, a fourth attempt at happily ever after, a fourth Cinderella attempt at being loved and cherished. It didn't seem likely that I would succeed. But this time it was different.

6

PRINCE NUMBER FOUR

I met Michael in a Dale Carnegie Course. He was a student and I was his group leader, which meant I was committed to support him throughout the 14 week course. I was so burnt out on men and failed marriages that I had personally sworn off men forever. I wanted nothing to do with any of them.

But Michael was charming and handsome with no pretense. He was from Kansas and what you saw, was what you got. It was easy to be with him and it didn't take long for him to break down my walls. He claimed to need "extra help" with the Dale Carnegie Course and therein began our relationship.

We started dating in April of 1983, when I cautiously introduced him to my son. I was afraid of letting anyone, who might end up leaving us, get close to Jesse. But Michael was different. I don't know if it was the stability that came from his Midwestern family values or something else, but he seemed safe. He seemed trustworthy. And beneath my conviction to never have another man in my life I was still desperately longing for that Cinderella story.

My relationship with Michael grew stronger every day and so it seemed did Michael's relationship with my little boy.

On my 26th birthday, when Jesse and I came home, Michael asked us to go into the bedroom, sit down on the bed and close our eyes. Jesse and I followed Michael's instructions. Jesse climbed up on the bed, and wiggled himself next to me in wonder. Nervously he squirmed as he covered his eyes, peeking out up at me and giggling. My heart was beating fast as I wrapped my arm around my son and closed my eyes.

Michael walked into the room, carrying a tray laden with a bottle of champagne, three chilled glasses, a gold ring that Michael had worn for the past 10 years and two red roses. Each rose was wrapped in frosted tissue paper with baby's breath and soft green ferns. "Okay, you can open your eyes now," Michael grinned.

First Michael handed me a rose saying, "Pamela, I love you. Will you be my wife?"

Still scarred by my past I was afraid to be hopeful and yet in the deepest places of my soul I wanted this to be THE ONE. I accepted the rose and with tears in my eyes I looked at Michael and said, "Yes."

Michael put the gold ring on my finger and Jesse clapped his little four year old hands and cheered, "Oh goodie!"

Next, Michael handed the other rose to Jesse and said, "Jesse, will you be my son?"

My sweet little boy dropped his head bashfully, and said, "Yes." That resulted in a lot of big smiles, happy tears and long hugs, followed by a toast to our new family. Jesse took one tiny sip of champagne and with a scrunched up face he declared, "That stuff is yuck."

As we began to make wedding plans, Michael suggested we be married in the Episcopal Church since that was the church he grew up in. This required that I complete a series of classes. I actively participated in the pre-marital course and earnestly studied, eager to learn more about God. I sincerely wanted to get this right before I entered marriage number four. With deep conviction, I resolved that I would never go through another divorce. No matter what – this was it for me. My marriage to Michael was going to be a triune marriage; not just Michael and me, this time it was God and Michael and me.

But despite all my promises, resolutions and knowing God really was part of our union, my marriage to Michael started out on the wrong foot. Shortly after we had sent out 300 wedding invitations, Michael confided that he was concerned about losing his job.

"Maybe we should postpone the wedding," Michael suggested. "Let's be sure our financial future is solid, before we jump into marriage."

I was so in love with Michael, and so desperate for stability, that I insisted that we go through with the wedding. What was money? "Don't worry," I told him. "I can make enough to support us." And the wedding went on as planned.

About a month after our wedding, Michael lost his job, and since I had promised him that this would not be a problem, he wasn't concerned when the next company he joined went belly up three months later. He didn't rush out to replace his job with something bigger or better. He just sort of washed his hands. Without saying it aloud, he effectively communicated, "You can handle this, so go for it."

With Michael's lack of concern for his unemployment, my respect for my new husband started to diminish. It was reminiscent of that time in the garage with Mom and Dad arguing over the radio. The challenge was tossed out and I resolved action. My problem-solving brain thought, "Okay – he lost his job – I have to double my efforts and take care of everyone." And that's just what I did.

From my perspective, Michael spent most of the next year, drinking beer, chewing tobacco and being a couch potato while I worked my freaking ass off. It's a bitter memory of our first year of marriage.

After my first round of Dale Carnegie Courses, I earned the promotion I sought to outside sales, selling commercial photographic equipment from Bakersfield to the Oregon border, while continuing to volunteer in the Dale Carnegie Courses. Eventually I made the switch and devoted all my energy to selling and teaching Dale Carnegie Courses.

To anyone on the outside, my marriage with Michael appeared good. We went to church together, but we were two people on different paths. A couple years into our marriage I learned that I was pregnant; we were both sort of startled to think that we had produced a child. During those first few years of marriage, Michael and I were going in different directions all the time. We barely acknowledged one another. It seemed impossible that we could have conceived a child. Michael suggested I get a second opinion.

My walk with God was peripheral back then. I knew God was there, but I hadn't surrendered everything to him. A big part of me recognized that He and I had a relationship, but I had other responsibilities I didn't share with God. I didn't yet know that I could trust God enough to let go of control. I didn't think Superwoman needed God to handle everything.

At first, the deeper I stepped into a personal relationship with God, the more I was surrounded with fear and apprehension. I had never done this before and my history made me feel that God might not accept me. Still, I persisted. My faith began to grow and I enthusiastically embraced the church. I served on the board, and contributed my leadership talents whenever needed. I bought a Life Application Study Bible, which helped me understand what the Bible was saying and how it applied to my life today. I had faith; it was nestled well in my intellect, and my world was wrapped in service to God and the church and taking care of everyone in my family. And then I attended my first Cursillo (cur-SEE-oh).

7

FROM MY HEAD TO MY HEART

I had accepted the Lord into my life, but I was still skeptical. I shudder to think of how I was during those tempestuous years. I wasn't reverent, I was glib. Sassily I'd say, "All right God, if you're really there, I need the phone to ring and an order to be there."

Oddly enough, despite my doubting attitude, and defiant challenges, often a half hour later, the phone would ring and there would be an order that I needed. I tested God like that, over and over for some years, and amazingly he consistently showed up. Even in my insolence, I couldn't deny that God was present and listening to me. I had to admit to myself that God was answering my prayers more frequently, consistently and beyond what I could consider a coincidence.

Then one day, a couple from our church offered to sponsor Michael and me to attend a Cursillo, an ecumenical Christian retreat that was held in the High Sierra. It's a short course in Christianity cloaked in a four day event that begins on Thursday evening and concludes on Sunday. It's described as an opportunity to strengthen faith and experience God's love through prayer, meditation, worship, fellowship, study, laughter, tears and unconditional love.

Our sponsors encouraged us to go, paid for all our expenses and even drove us into the remote area where the retreat was held. We thought they were going to stay for the weekend with us, but instead they dropped us off, and drove away. Immediately, I was completely out of my comfort zone. As I watched their car fade into the distance, I felt a flutter of panic in my heart; if I didn't like this, I had no way to escape.

After we were settled in our respective dorm rooms, one of the first activities of the event involved walking the "Stations of the Cross," which is a 14-step devotion that commemorates Jesus' last day on Earth as a man. It's practiced in both Catholic and Protestant churches around the world. Fourteen stations are placed around a church, garden, or meeting room with artwork that depicts the specific events of his last day, beginning with his condemnation.

Here at the retreat, the stations were marked around the grounds, with original pen & ink watercolors created by a local artist that instantly grabbed my attention. As an artist myself, I related to these images far more than the stained glass windows in church. They resonated deep within my soul.

The fourteen steps are: 1) Jesus is condemned to death; 2) Jesus takes up his cross; 3) Jesus falls the first time; 4) Jesus meets his mother; 5) the cross is laid on Simon of Cyrene; 6) a woman wipes the face of Jesus; 7) Jesus falls a second time; 8) Jesus meets the women of Jerusalem; 9) Jesus falls a third time; 10) Jesus is stripped of his garments; 11) Jesus is nailed to the cross; 12) Jesus dies on the cross; 13) the body of Jesus is placed in the arms of his mother; 14) Jesus is laid in the tomb.

Michael and I began walking in the dark, station to station, looking at the artwork with a flashlight, and listening to the message for each station. When we came to the stop where Mary, the mother of Jesus, was watching her son be crucified, the message of that station struck my heart.

Mary is speaking:

"Today, as I remember him lying on the cross, with his arms outstretched, it is the sound of the hammer hitting the nails that stays with me. I remember pulling the first of many wood splinters from his fingers as a child working in Joseph's shop. Against his precious hands and wrists, that touched and healed so many, a nail was placed, and a hammer pounded the nail through his flesh and into the wood of the cross. The sound - metal against metal - that ring - and the look on his face - the spasm of his whole body - I will never forget. Then, the other hand and finally his feet are nailed to the cross. Spend some time with him now, imagining how they lifted him up on the cross, nailed there, that you might be free."

I was stunned. God had become Mary's child. He had come to earth to live as one of us and to die so that we could be reconciled to him. A chill ran up my spine as I thought about my own little boys, whom I loved and treasured with all my heart. It hit me, right between the eyes – would I ever consider sending one of my sons to a world that hated him? Would I send him to his death? Would I send him to a horrible, brutal, violent death because I wanted a relationship with people who didn't even love me?

It blew my mind. It was a life changing moment. In my heart, I realized the incredible level of sacrifice God made for me. And within that moment, my relationship with God became even more personal.

Questions began swimming in my mind. Who is this God that would sacrifice someone so precious, his very own child, his very self...for a bunch of people who hated him? For people who couldn't care less about him? Who was this God that loved me at this inconceivable level? And what did I need to do to be fully in a relationship with him?

Suddenly, the search for God had moved from my head to my heart. I was humbled and honored by God's sacrifice. Why would He do that for me, a smart aleck, cynical skeptic? I felt like I'd stepped on the end of a rake and been hit square between the eyes by the handle. This new reality resonated deep within my soul. I could hardly even talk about God without crying, I felt so broken by what he had done for me, and how undeserving I was to receive this gift.

I was riveted throughout the rest of the Cursillo event. It was an experience of the most intense, inclusive love I had ever received and something that I had been looking for all my life – total, unconditional love. I was loved here, without performing, just for being me. The retreat provided for every detail – authentic speakers, well planned activities, excellent meals, hilarious skits and meaningful teaching. Every time I would return to my bed, I'd find an anonymous love gift on my pillow. They called it "palanca".

I was surrounded by love.

When I came back home from the event, I was hungry for a deeper relationship than my snarky disrespectful attitude had previously allowed. My prayer life went far deeper than my, "Well, God, if you're there..." to a solid communication wrapped in awe, respect and love. I began journaling to God, pouring out my heart on paper.

I was also determined to pay it forward. I was privileged to serve on several different Cursillo teams and as often as possible Michael and I sponsored others to attend Cursillos. Most importantly, I started building a solid relationship with God.

Deeper and deeper I studied the Bible and the more I did the more I learned about God's character. I learned he was a trustworthy heavenly Father. As I read story after story I grew to love him and that drove me to want nothing less than a right relationship with him. I became grateful and no longer skeptical. I went from taunting God to make the phone ring, to reverently whispering, "God, I know you love me, and that you are here with me. You know my needs and I'm thanking you now, for the results you will provide, whatever you are going to bring my way." I stopped telling God what to do, and opened my mind to the enormous possibilities at his disposal.

It wasn't magic, and my life didn't suddenly become rich, meaningful and without stress. There was still a struggle to feel loved at home. Michael and I were on the same path now, but in two different lanes. No matter how well I did at work, I always felt like I had to do more and do it better. It seemed that while I had been striving to be enough on my own terms, only on the mountaintops of a Cursillo event had I tasted what I longed for. I was still anesthetizing myself with alcohol just to stay numb, to avoid emotional pain and to ease the pain of a mysterious illness. I knew God loved me, but it was not integrated into the fabric of who I was because I lived a duality of life. I was straddling the fence between the way I had lived in the past and the life God was offering me now. I still felt that I had to perform; I had to be available to whoever needed me, whenever called, always taking care of other people, rather than taking care of myself. I never even made it on the list.

8

A WRONG TURN

I drew deeply into my faith as I studied God's Word. I became a leader for Cursillo. Being a leader of a four day event took months of planning, team building, decision making and a huge time commitment. But it was satisfying to watch God work in the lives of the team and the participants and my faith grew with each event.

And then one Cursillo evening, something life changing happened that sent me into a tailspin of unimaginable proportions. At each Cursillo, on the second evening of the retreat, there was an optional healing service offered. I had attended healing services at past Cursillos but this time I distinctly remember thinking, "Hmmm, I don't have anything that needs healing." But since I was there, I figured a little extra healing could never hurt, so I decided that I would ask for prayer for my career. I was working in real estate then, and I really wanted to leave that industry. This would be a good opportunity to bring that before God.

The healing service was held in a large room, warmly lit with candles and soft guitar music. The room was packed with people and an empty chair was placed in the center of the room. A woman sat down on the chair, and Pastor Aaron, who was in charge of the service, asked her about her prayer request. Then Aaron placed his hands on her head, and several people gathered around her to lay their hands on her shoulders to pray together with the minister. As soon as the prayer was completed, the next person would sit in the chair, tell Aaron the prayer request and he would pray with the others surrounding them. This continued as one after another sat in the chair, requesting healing prayers.

When it was my turn, I walked up to the chair and sat down. I hardly knew Pastor Aaron but I said, "I would like prayer for career guidance."

Aaron smiled and said, "Okay." He placed his hands on my head and the others reached out to touch me as Aaron began to pray. I was stunned when instead of career guidance, Aaron prayed for the healing of my intimate relationships.

I almost jumped up to stop him. Was he nuts? Was he still praying for the person who had just left the chair? I didn't need this prayer – I needed guidance for my career. Still, he kept praying for intimate and emotional healing. I sat there, rigid and tense, my heart beating, I'm sure visibly, through my sweater. As Aaron finished, I jumped up and swiftly headed for the door. I couldn't get out of that room fast enough.

It took Aaron awhile to finish praying for the entire room, but when he did, he came looking for me. I wasn't angry with Aaron, I just didn't understand why he prayed what he did.

"Pamela," Aaron said kindly, "I know you asked for career help, but the only thing I could see when I touched your head was the need for healing in your heart. That's why I prayed for healing of intimate relationships."

I stared at him blankly, wondering how he could have gotten his signals so poorly crossed.

"Does that make any sense to you?" Aaron pushed me.

"Ha!" I thought. Did that make any sense to me? I said, "Maybe," then I walked out into the night air alone.

My spirit was stirring, and my thoughts were a jumble of denial and hope. Did healing of intimate relationships mean anything to me? The Wonder Woman of production, perfection and success? The woman who had three broken marriages behind her and a crumbling fourth in her midst? Healing for intimate relationships?

I hardly slept that night, but I know I must have fallen asleep, because when I woke up the next morning, it was as if I had landed in Oz. I felt like Dorothy when she opened the door and walked out of the black and gray world into living Technicolor. Everything was brighter, colors more richly saturated, bird songs more melodic, the sunshine wrapping me in penetrating warmth. All of my sentient parts were tingling and I felt so alive. It was a glorious revelation. It was startling to recall how many times throughout my life I had locked away the parts of me that felt emotions, always trying to block out the pain.

Aaron could see my joy that morning, and suggested that Michael and I might consider attending an Intimacy Workshop. This sounded perfect to me and the hope that began to build in me was permeating my heart.

After the weekend I went home and tried to explain to Michael what had happened at the healing service. He nodded, placating me, but he didn't understand just how profound the healing was to my spirit. His reaction made me feel as if I didn't exist.

"Michael," I broached him carefully. "Would you consider going to an Intimacy Workshop with me?"

He didn't look up from his magazine, just nodded and said, "Sure, we can do that, when we have the money." His comment implied that we would never have the money for something like that.

My big, bright balloon of hope was instantly popped. I was devastated. I wanted nothing more than to feel loved and cherished and valued, and the hope I had of achieving it had just been dismissed. On auto-pilot, I headed straight for the kitchen to mix up an extra tall gin and tonic. I plopped three ice cubes into the glass and as I began to open the gin bottle, I realized that I hadn't mixed this faithful mind-numbing medication for a while. It had been a twice daily fix for many years, but I hadn't felt the need for self-medicating alcohol since before the retreat.

The veil of denial was starting to lift. Standing there, on the checkered black and white tile floor in the kitchen, I realized that I had been hiding from the pain in my life for a long time. I put the top back on the gin and filled my glass with water. I didn't mix the drink. I decided that I wanted to walk through this experience feeling everything God was going to show me.

I took my ice water outside to the back yard and sat down on a patio chair. I began thinking back to my earliest memories when I was continually looking for love or affirmation that I was valuable. I thought about how I had been so let down in that goal, that I chose not to feel at all. I had gone so long without feeling loved or gaining confirmation of my worth that I had locked up the sensors to feel that pain. It was how I coped and I did it well. I would push down the negative feelings, grab a hold of my boot straps and move on to be the world's best caretaker, producer, provider, or whatever the job required. And now, I could see that this feeling alive was what God wanted for me, and it started with healing my intimate relationships.

But I handled it completely the wrong way. Musing what I was to do, I still did what was right in my own eyes.

Caleb was a professional colleague from work. We held business seminars together, and enjoyed a positive, mutual respect for one another. I remembered that he and his wife had previously attended Cursillo. They were familiar with the healing service that was offered. So one day, after a business lunch, I told Caleb about my experience at the Cursillo. I confided in him that Michael and I were still walking different directions in our path toward intimacy. Caleb was sympathetic and a good listener, and even admitted to me that he and his wife were equally disconnected. We continued the conversation later in the week over another business lunch and the more we talked, the more we understood each other.

Then one day, somehow, Caleb and I experienced a passionate kiss and the sparks flew. Honestly, I thought we were going to catch on fire. The passion I had always dreamed of, that Prince Charming kind of passion, had ignited and I was full blown in love on the spot. I abandoned my marriage vows and crossed the big line with Caleb to find the intimacy I so deeply longed for.

I knew it was wrong. Caleb knew it was wrong, but we justified it as two people who were desperate for love. I even tried to convince myself that this was what God wanted for me, a special healing perhaps. But I knew deep in my heart, that wasn't true. As a Christian leader, this was totally against living as a citizen of the Kingdom of God. I struggled with guilt every day knowing I had crossed the bounds of my faith. Even more of a concern was the impact this would have on our families. But it didn't stop me.

Caleb and I still found dozens of ways to be together. It wasn't just the physical relationship we enjoyed; we talked for hours about our dreams, our goals, and what our ideal life would be. Like teenagers we were both deeply into our fantasy love affair, discounting the carnage in our wake. I reasoned with God, asking, "Why would you unlock this door to my heart and let this man step in only to wrench it away and leave me longing again?"

I can still feel the blinders that I had on, and how gently God removed them, to show me the truth. It was at a Cursillo Ultreya gathering, where participants of previous retreats come back for a reunion when I began to feel remorse for my affair. I felt dirty and shame-filled yet grateful for the love and intimacy I had experienced, because I thought it was what I had always longed for. I prayed for forgiveness. I never wanted to hurt anyone. I just wanted to feel loved. Could I ever find that now with Michael?

After three months of a fantasy love adventure, Caleb and I ended our affair. Ironically, the next day was Valentine's Day. Michael and I were in the living room of our home when I confessed to him that I had been having an affair for the past three months. I kept it as short and simple as I could. Michael asked questions and I answered them succinctly. I was emotionless. I didn't have any feelings for Michael. He asked more questions, and I began preparing myself to be kicked to the curb. In my heart I thought, "There goes marriage number four."

9

HOPELESS AND ALONE

It had been a few days since I'd confessed to Michael about the affair I had ended with Caleb. I missed the relationship but there was no going back to it. I had no idea what Michael was thinking, he was so distant and avoided me at all costs. I felt hopeless and alone and without direction. I decided to talk to Pastor Aaron about it.

Feeling dazed and heartsick, I climbed into my Subaru station wagon and whipped the seatbelt across my chest, jamming the clasp into the lock. Despite the warm sunlight pouring in through the windshield I felt cold; chilled to the bone. Was it from the brisk winter day or the hard shell closing in around my heart?

I started the engine, and began weaving my way out of my suburban neighborhood, into the rural country roads that thread through the Sierra foothills. I wasn't even sure why I was going to see Pastor Aaron. Despite the crooked road and steep hills, I began driving faster - straightening out the mountainous curves, as I felt my heart squeeze in pain. I finally understood; it was just one more lesson I had learned from the school of hard knocks. I knew why some people chose to kill themselves. Sometimes...the pain is simply unbearable.

I crossed over the center line, slamming my foot on the brake just enough to complete the curve. I accelerated hard as the car roared up the next hill, and I reflected over the last few months. I'd experienced some of the highest highs and lowest lows of my lifetime and now everything was crashing in on me. My life had become a pattern of despair, panic and regret. I couldn't stand it anymore.

I kept driving, ignoring the wild turkeys along the road, and the deer in the meadow. I was completely engulfed in my regret. For as long as I could remember, I had guarded my heart; always leaving before I could be abandoned. It worked well for me. I worked hard at keeping pain and loneliness at bay. But this time was different. This time God was in the mix.

I thought about how easy it would be to end it all right there. If I pressed hard on the gas pedal as I came around the next bend, I could fly off the road and just be done.

But then my "cynical part," who'd been showing up more and more often lately, countered in my head, saying, "With your luck you'd just wreck the car and not finish the job. Then you'd be in an even bigger mess."

So I kept driving. I slowed enough to make the sharp turns, but continued to exceed the speed limits along the country road. The ache inside my heart was so deep; I could hardly breathe.

How did I get here? It felt as though I'd been trying so hard for so long to just feel loved and safe. I climbed ladders of success for years, but I didn't find love there. The pain of another loss was testing the limits of my threshold.

Most of my life I'd been characterized as "Positive Pamela," but now, I couldn't find even a flicker of optimism. Darkness enveloped me like never before. I'd suffered with depression most of my life but this was different. I couldn't keep faking it.

As I continued driving my mind whirled around all of my stress. I had worked tenaciously to make the best life I could for myself, and from a certain perspective one could make a case that I had succeeded. But my success was a facade, a skillfully built house of cards that was now tumbling down all around me. I just wanted to disappear.

Only days before I had delivered a fatal blow to my fourth marriage. Deja Vu. And I knew what was ahead. I could see it all - the telling and retelling of "my side." The defending, the shame, the division of property, as well as friends and family. And my children… Oh how I wanted to protect them from this. The carnage was deep and the desperation saturated my heart and soul.

I pulled into the church parking lot, and wandered into the office. As soon as I sat down in Aaron's study, he could see that my "light" had faded. Just a few months before, at that healing service at Cursillo, Aaron had been a conduit for a revelation that abruptly changed my life. But now the light of that hope had diminished to a pile of ashes.

"I can't do it anymore," I told Aaron. "I just want to die. It's hopeless." I confessed to Aaron the affair I'd been having. In no uncertain terms he told me that if I continued with Caleb it would lead to disaster.

Then Pastor Aaron looked at me with kindness and genuine compassion. He leaned in and locked eyes with me. "Pamela, I want you to think about the pain you are feeling. Just how deep is it?" I felt his eyes pulling at me and I looked out the window, with tears rolling down my cheeks, shaking my head silently. I couldn't even answer him.

Aaron continued, "Think about your pain, Pamela. Now multiply it by 1000."

Trembling, I looked back at him in bewilderment and stared at Aaron, not understanding why he would let me imagine an even deeper level of heartache than I was already suffering.

And then he said, "That is the kind of pain your children will feel if you do this."

His words slapped me. WHAM! My children. My beautiful boys. There was no one and nothing I cared more about in this world than my dear boys. In that instant, suicide came off the table. And with untold resolve, I knew that I would have to face this mess head on.

10

A NEW BEGINNING

When I returned home, I found Michael withdrawn and quiet. I gathered the courage to ask him what he was thinking. Michael acknowledged that he had the right to divorce me and I knew that he felt cheated out of the life we had once hoped to have together. Michael was processing his pain and grief and became bitter. Bits of encouragement from him felt more like blackmail than love. He would say things like, "Well, I probably won't tell anyone unless such and such happens," or "You know what you'll do to our children if you do this again."

There was a lot of blaming from Michael, and I had it coming. I could not fault him for his reaction. I could see that he was angry, but still trying to come to terms with my betrayal. There was also a softening too. Michael told me that as he prayed about it and thought about our family, he wanted to try to save our marriage.

"I have always loved you, Pamela," Michael said with tears in his eyes. "I just haven't liked you very much for a long time."

I could hardly believe it. I had already divorced Michael emotionally and I never would have guessed that he would still want me. Now I had to re-engage. I thought about my commitment to God in my marriage and how I had told God I would stay in the game if he would just show me some kind of progress.

With Michael's announcement that he wanted our marriage to work, we decided to try some counseling. I knew from my readings in the Song of Songs, that God intended marriage to be an amazing, beautiful partnership. I reasoned that he wouldn't want me to stay in this fractured, lifeless relationship as it was. So with trepidation, I began to break the cycle.

I stopped running away from problems and pain and ran straight into God's arms. Step by painfully tiny step, we made progress. My motivation was still fantasy passion, while Michael's was keeping the family together. I wish I could say that I embraced the challenge God had in store for me with boldness and courage. But the next few months were harder than I could have imagined.

After my chat with Aaron, I knew that suicide wasn't an option, because of my boys. But I began to think that if I could make my death look natural or like an accident, it might be a suitable solution. Other times I would only think of myself, and mentally plot ways to just make the pain and sadness go away. I had betrayed Michael, and I feared that he would never love me. One night, at a prayer vigil I found myself seriously considering taking a whole bunch of pills right there at the church and just going to sleep. I was ready to give up, and in my despair, I wasn't capable of thinking of others, even my children. But God didn't give up on me.

And then, true to his word, Michael found a counselor who offered an intimacy workshop. It was a three day, "make it or break it" clinic, where we could try to put our relationship back together.

Our workshop started on a Friday night. Normally there were three or four couples on a weekend like this, but on our particular weekend, it turned out that Michael and I were the only ones. The first thing the counselor had us complete was a Myers Briggs personality assessment.

The assessment revealed me as an "ENFP", The Champion. This personality type is creative, people-centered and full of contagious enthusiasm for new ideas, people and projects. Michael was an "ISTJ", The Inspector. His type is responsible, organized and driven to create order. The test revealed what we already knew. Michael and I had completely opposite personality styles. The counselor told us that in 20 years of administering this test, he had never seen two people more diametrically opposite than me and Michael.

I could have told him that. I wasn't encouraged.

But then the counselor said, "You two are either going to have the marriage from hell (been there, done that), or you're going to have the most rich marriage anyone can hope for. You have the entire spectrum of possibilities covered."

My spark of hope reignited. At that point he gave us an assignment. He sent us on a grocery shopping trip. The rules were clear – each of us would shop the way we liked to shop, and the other would observe without comment. I knew this would be funny. Michael shops with a list, in order of the rows he will walk down, starting with the door of the store that he will enter. He will buy everything on the list, and waste no time looking at anything not on the list. Michael's shopping style is quick and efficient – in and out and on budget.

I, on the other hand, am stimulated by my environment. I might take a shopping list, to remind me of what I need, but I wander through the fresh flowers, taking in the mix of fragrances, and then I stop at the produce section, admiring the rich vibrance of the bright red berries, the vivid orange Mandarins and the wide variety of greens scattered amongst the vegetables. I am attracted to the beauty of a grocery store, and for me there is so much more happening than just selecting things to eat. I flit all over the place, enjoying the ambiance.

This first night was my turn. Michael was to just walk with me and observe my process. On our next shopping trip, we would do it Michael's way.

Michael and I were surprised that despite our different approaches, we ended up accomplishing the same things, at about the same price, as we checked our list later. It was interesting that we behaved so completely different in a simple task. This exercise was the beginning of introducing us to a new concept – **just because we do something differently doesn't mean it's wrong.**

This was a significant lesson we applied on multiple levels. We are different, but neither one is wrong.

Saturday morning we met again with the counselor and he had us sit in a knee to knee triangle with him.

"Today you are each going to talk, while the other listens, without interruption," the counselor said. "When I talk with Michael, Pamela, I want you to listen, really listen to his answers, but no speaking."

I braced myself. With my past, and in my previous counseling sessions I was routinely thrown under the bus. I was always the bad girl, everything was always my fault. I was ready for that. So I was surprised at his first question for Michael.

"Michael," the counselor began deliberately, "How often do you think about your wife?"

That was a loaded question! I thought Michael would say something like, "At least quarterly," since that's when we filed our taxes. But instead, with a crack in his voice, Michael replied, "I think about her every hour of every day."

I was stunned. I couldn't believe it. I pushed my skepticism down and waited for more questions.

"Michael, what do you believe your role as husband should look like?" The counselor looked directly at Michael, and encouraged him with a smile.

Michael began describing the husband I've always wanted: a strong family leader, good provider, tender lover, a man who cherished his family. Michael was the man I had dreamed of, he just didn't know how to get there. I was blown away. Never in a million years did I anticipate that Michael actually loved me. I certainly hadn't been feeling his love for a very long time. I was shocked.

That revelation, cracked my shell a little bit. I kept listening and learned more about what Michael wanted to do in our marriage. I was astonished that Michael's hopes and dreams were perfectly in line with mine. I was elated, because suddenly I knew there was hope.

Then the counselor reversed the questioning, and while Michael listened without speaking, he asked me questions. It was a major breakthrough, as Michael and I learned that we weren't as different as we thought we were.

Michael learned that I felt as if I had been carrying a heavy burden of the finances in our marriage. Up to that point, Michael had been mostly unemployed or under employed. For the first time, I really heard how Michael believed that I had set him up for failure as the family bread winner, since right before our marriage, being fearful of losing his job, he had wanted to postpone our wedding and I insisted that I could provide for us, even without his income.

The counseling session provided a safe way for us to air years' worth of stuffed pain without interruption. It allowed both of us to see the real pain, dig to the root of all of it and understand one another. By the end of the weekend I had regained a small amount of respect for my husband. I thought it was God's way of saying to me, "See Pamela, I'm showing you progress. It will take a while. Just hang in there."

I was still bargaining with God. "Okay God," I answered him. "I'll stay in the game as long as you show me progress." Even though my faith was growing I was still miles from maturity.

We continued with our counselor over the next several months, with lots of other exercises. We came back once a week to meet and check our progress. We were finally communicating, and coming up with strategies for fixing the big things that were broken.

Michael and I both took the counseling commitment seriously. The counselor routinely assigned homework, and when things got rocky, we'd call him mid-week and he'd talk us down, get us back on track and working together again. This pattern continued for months, before we could make it from one week to the next without needing his help in between.

Through this process, a spark of love ignited in me for Michael. I began to feel as if I had the tools in place for calling on the Holy Spirit whenever I felt tempted to be indifferent to Michael. I started to appreciate our different approaches to just about everything. After six months, we stopped seeing the therapist on a weekly basis, but kept him on speed dial when needed.

Michael and I wanted to get back into a church family. We joined a different congregation and began to intentionally put God in the middle of our relationship. We joined small groups to deepen our faith and apply our new found understanding of God in practical ways. When we changed churches, we were completely honest with our new priest, explaining that we had reconciled our marriage. We wanted to start fresh and grow. The new priest suggested that Michael and I join separate small groups – Michael a men's group and that I join a women's group. It was wise counsel and both Michael and I began to grow in the Lord.

As a couple, we began praying, reading the Bible and growing in our faith. I could hardly believe how profoundly a nearby men's Promise Keepers (PK) conference would impact Michael.

PK is 'a Christ-centered organization dedicated to instilling a passion in men to hear, obey and daily meditate on the Word of God'. Since 1990, when PK first began, they have impacted the lives of more than 7 million men.

When Michael attended his first PK event he came home more broken than I'd ever seen him. Up until that point, I had carried most of the weight of my affair squarely on my shoulders. But when Michael returned from Promise Keepers, he told me that he wanted me to become a Promise "Reaper." He got down on his knees and with tears in his eyes, asked me to forgive him for not providing for our family, for not nurturing a loving relationship and for not loving me better. It was a remarkable moment. "Wow," I thought. "Someone else is finally going to share the heavy lifting in this relationship."

This simple act, strengthened our marriage a lot. It increased our connection to one another, and I started to feel compassion and love for Michael. But the most important change was that I had a solid respect for him. Respect was what I had lost and when Michael came back from that conference and owned those things, my respect meter shot to the sky.

But Michael didn't stop with words, he continued to demonstrate those characteristics in his daily life. His interest in me grew and we became closer than we had ever been.

11

SLAYING THE MONEY GIANT

Communication and Finances. The two most common issues that frequently derail marriages... Michael and I worked hard together with a counselor, to learn to communicate with each other. But it was God who spoke to us directly about money.

As my faith continued to grow, I could see God showing up in all facets of my life. My experiences at Cursillo events were affirming that the peace I had found was through the Lord. I was so enthusiastic, grateful and on fire. I wanted to tell everyone I knew about what God can do with a trashed life, but I knew that I had to be sensitive in my sharing. A more mature believer advised me to *talk with God about my friends before I talk to my friends about God.* It was good advice. I had learned to lean on God for almost everything in my life, and the more I counted on him, the more things improved. Except with our finances.

Michael and I had struggled financially since the beginning of our marriage when he lost his job. His "career path" looked more like a map of county roads, crisscrossing one another, some making sharp turns and others hitting dead ends, than it did a healthy resume. He had tried many jobs but never felt satisfied so he jumped from one to another for years. I worked as an Independent Contractor in a self-employed, commission-based, career with no base paycheck arriving each month. We didn't know how much our income would be from month to month, and in the tumultuous real estate market back then, as many sales would fall out of escrow as would actually close. Michael and I lived on credit. We suffered the consequences of financial mismanagement with bankruptcy, cars repossessed, home foreclosure and federal tax liens. Even with God in our marriage and our communication improving daily, Michael and I fought about money – a lot.

Michael had been raised in a structured family with a mom who carefully managed their finances and taught her boys to do the same. Michael was a saver. Budgeting was a natural part of life. When it came to gift giving in Michael's family, a sincere card was usually the most that was exchanged.

I, on the other hand, had been raised to believe that credit cards were essentially free money and whenever life got hard, retail therapy was a ready solution. As for gift giving, I watched my mom give generously to everyone… Whether we had money or not, mom would buy gifts for nearly every person she had ever met on every occasion that Hallmark celebrated. "Budget" was a nasty word, rarely spoken in our household.

God was there in our marriage, but the reality was that I still hadn't totally surrendered to him. He had most of me but I didn't want to share my finances with him.

Then, in the early 90's, I went to a conference in Oregon with our church leadership team. There were an array of excellent speakers with messages that encouraged my faith and touched my heart. One speaker talked about the Bible story of David and Goliath. David was a young shepherd boy, who with the help of God, killed an invincible evil giant warrior, with a simple stone and a sling.

The speaker looked out into the audience and said, "We all have Goliath in our lives. We all face obstacles that seem huge and impossible to overcome. All of us have big problems that we are unable to solve on our own. But with God, all things are possible."

The speaker paused and let that sink in for a moment and then said, "David took down Goliath with one small stone, because he turned his problem over to God. What is the Goliath in your life that you need to turn over to God?"

The auditorium seated about 2000 people, and since there were only about 100 of us attending the conference, we were asked to spread out around the auditorium. As the lights were turned down to create a more private, intimate setting, the speaker said, "Now, I want you to ask God to show you the Goliaths in your life."

As I sat in that dimly lit auditorium, kneeling between a couple of pews, I took a deep breath and whispered, "Okay, God, what do you want me to learn here? What are my Goliaths?" In a few moments, like a familiar stirring of energy, I received a message in my spirit. Just as clearly as if he'd spoken in an audible voice I heard, "intimacy and finances."

That really wasn't a surprise. Michael and I had been working hard on the intimacy issue and with God in our marriage, we were making great progress. I thought about the mess of our financial situation back home. The mound of debt and unpaid bills was staggering; the tax liens were overwhelming and there was a multitude of other fallout associated with our financial disaster. That was a Goliath for sure.

So I pressed God, "What do you want to teach me? Why am I here?"

And then God gave me a startling message, "I want you to trust me with your finances. I want you to begin tithing. Immediately."

I laughed out loud, in that quiet auditorium. I was certain that I did not hear that message correctly.

"But God," I argued, "We can hardly make enough money to live on. We can't pay our taxes, or put new tires on the car, I need every penny to survive! You want ten percent? You can't be serious."

But God, in his gentle, patient way was very clear. It was one of those "red phone moments," where God got right in my face. "Yes," I heard him reply. "And I want you to start doing it immediately."

In that instant, I was 100 percent convinced this was God's voice and God's instruction. My Goliath was finances and like David, I was unarmed to slay this giant on my own. But with God, all things are possible.

It was a mind boggling revelation. I wanted to obey this request from God, but I was married and this was not my decision to make alone. Michael and I were financially dysfunctional, so how could I even explain this new logic to him? How could I tell Michael that I planned to give away ten percent of my next check, right off the top?

I called Michael from my hotel room, and tried to explain my incredible God moment.

"It was so clear, and so real. I can't disobey God's direction," I explained with a trembling voice. I tried to describe all the details, so Michael would have a better understanding of my God encounter.

"I understand that you had a special message from God, Pamela," Michael said calmly. "But you can't be serious about giving ten percent of our meager income to the church right off. Honey, we can't make ends meet as it is. I think we need to be practical about this. Let's talk more about it when you get home."

We chatted a bit further, with me being excited and persuasive and Michael being composed and rational. Finally I said, "Honey, you can do whatever you want with your income, but I cannot ignore the message God gave me." Michael acknowledged my conviction and said, "We'll give it some thought."

I went home from the conference, still fired up about my face to face message from God. I explained to Michael about my desire to put God in our finances the same as we had put God in our marriage. Together we began looking to the Bible for answers. Michael started reading what God says about tithing and in the midst of our financial crisis I knew that was a good sign. We didn't know how we would pay the rent that month, and God's direction was to give ten percent of our income to him first. Both of us felt anxious, but we were committed to trusting God, despite common sense pointing us in the opposite direction.

In the book of Malachi, God says this: "'Will a mere mortal rob God? Yet you rob me. 'But you ask, "How are we robbing you?" 'In tithes and offerings. You are under a curse – your whole nation – because you are robbing me. Bring the whole tithe into the storehouse, that there may be food in my house. Test me in this,' says the Lord Almighty, 'and see if I will not throw open the floodgates of heaven and pour out so much

blessing that there will not be room enough to store it."
Malachi 3:8-10

It is the only place in the bible where God says, "Test me in this." With that, Michael and I agreed to try it. "Okay," Michael said, "Let's trust him."

So timidly, but with resolve, we started tithing and that was an absolute turning point in our lives financially. Since Michael and I made that decision, and stuck with it, we have never been without. Time and again, we would find ourselves in a hopeless situation, unable to pay a bill…and a mysterious check would show up in the mailbox or an escrow I had given up on would close. God has continued to bless us beyond our wildest expectations. We became completely faithful to tithing and have never looked back. Without fail, it's one of the best things we've ever done.

It taught me two important lessons. First, **God is seldom early, but never late** and secondly, **you simply cannot out-give God**. We keep trying and God just keeps blessing us, over and over and over.

12

NINE PAGES OF UGLY

As an adult, I changed addresses many times. Some of the moving was from husband to husband, some was job related and often moving was financially motivated. Putting down roots was not in the cards. When Michael and I were first married, we lived near the end of a cul-de-sac in a three bedroom, two bath duplex in Carmichael, a comfortable Sacramento suburb. The duplex had a small yard for my four year old son to play and it was a good place for us to get started in our life together. We lived there until I was pregnant with my second son, Trevor.

When I was 9 months pregnant, I left my job at Dale Carnegie for maternity leave. Michael was unemployed again and in desperation we moved into my mom's house. It was horrible. Michael's pride was wounded by his inability to provide for our family, I was hormonal and to make it worse, Mom was just mean to Michael. I felt like I was between a rock and a hard place, needing somewhere to stay with a new baby on the way and yet wanting to honor Michael's feelings as well. Fortunately, we didn't stay there long, just until Trevor was about three months old and we moved into a town house.

A few years later, Michael and I had saved enough to purchase our first home. The California real estate prices were sky high back then, and all we could afford on our budget was a sweet little stone house. It had been one of the original homesteads in Citrus Heights, made of stones 18 inches thick; to us it was a fairytale cottage and we loved it. We made some great memories with our boys in that home but eventually we agreed that we needed more room, so we leased our little stone house, with an option to buy, to a couple of women, and we moved to a larger home in Arden Park, closer to our church.

Our real estate investment took a hit when the women stopped paying their rent and wrecked our fairytale cottage. This forced us to try to make the house payments on the little stone house, as well as our lease payments on the Arden Park house. It wasn't long before the little stone house was being foreclosed on, and our family had to move out of our Arden Park house because we couldn't afford all the money going out.

Once again Michael and I moved our family, this time into a small rental house. I was working in real estate, and I knew that the best way to resolve our situation was to sell the stone house before the foreclosure proceedings.

I launched an exhaustive sales campaign to sell our little cottage, showing it numerous times, but it did not sell. Part of the problem was that a buyer would have to pay $25,000 cash up front. On a positive note, there was a desirable FHA loan that could be assumed if the buyer qualified. I kept calling out to God, asking Him to intervene as the foreclosure date drew close. Finally, defeated, I resigned myself to the foreclosure. That sweet little fairytale cottage had become an anchor chained around my neck and we decided to just let the house go to auction.

But God had a better idea. The day before the foreclosure, I received a phone call at my office. A man was interested in the house. I didn't jump for joy or celebrate. In fact, I was rather crass.

"Well, you should know there is a second mortgage that has to be paid in cash, up front," I blurted out. "Do you have $25,000 in cash? If not, I don't have time to show the property." This certainly wasn't a sales technique I had learned in my Dale Carnegie training. I was so discouraged; I had given up on selling the property.

"Yes I do have $25,000," the buyer said. "I'd like to look at the house today."

I paused, but I didn't get excited. The foreclosure was the next day. "Okay," I replied. "What time do you want to meet?"

Within hours we had a signed sales agreement, a cashier's check for $25,000 and the buyer had assumed our FHA loan!

What a miracle! We had avoided foreclosure on that house with no time to spare. The house was sold, and the problem was resolved. But unfortunately with all the circumstances that brought us to this point, our credit report did not look good at all.

In reality, our credit report was nine pages of ugly, and followed us for a while, making Michael and I ineligible to qualify for a home loan. As a realtor, I knew the value of investing in a home, but I also knew that lenders would never consider providing a loan to us with all the derogatory items listed in our credit history. So Michael and I continued to rent our small home in a quiet, friendly neighborhood.

When Trevor started first grade, he was identified as a gifted child. His teacher told us that Trevor was often bored in his traditional classroom. Michael and I knew Trevor was bright, but we were surprised that he was being disruptive in class because of it. We decided to move Trevor to a rapid learner program in a different school within the district and began looking for a house to rent in that neighborhood.

As we set out, we prayed, "God, show us the way. Lead us to the home you have already prepared in advance for us." God was now in charge of our finances and it was going to take a miracle to find a house we could afford.

Michael pulled out the Thomas Bros. map book and identified the pages that covered the area around the rapid learner school. We hopped in the car and started driving through the neighborhoods, looking for a house to rent. We found lots of homes for sale, but our credit report reminded me not to even slow down in front of those homes. I knew what kind of credit a buyer had to have to qualify for a home loan, and I knew for sure that we didn't have it. Prior to turning our finances over to God we had been through financial nightmare after nightmare, and in the recent real estate market, I was lucky to close half my escrows. On top of everything else, we now had a whopping $22,000 in accumulated tax liens. Michael and I had been using every penny we earned just to pay the bills. We didn't have money to pay taxes, and I knew that on paper, we still looked really bad.

We continued our drive further around the neighborhood, when we stumbled onto a hidden lane, where a DIY sign read, "For Sale, By Owner." It was obscure and we would have surely missed it if God hadn't abruptly prompted me to look over my shoulder as we were driving by.

I wrote down the phone number. "Maybe if it's for sale by owner, they would consider a lease with an option to buy," I suggested to Michael. That ugly credit report was in my briefcase, as we headed back to tour the property.

The house had three bedrooms, one of which was a master suite. There was also a garage that had been converted into a huge bedroom/playroom for the little boys who lived there, as well as a comfortable living room, dining room, a country kitchen and more space than I had ever imagined for our family. The property was raw, but the house was beautiful. With two thirds of an acre, the property had a ton of potential. There was even the beginning of a perfect garden area.

Michael withheld his excitement but I know he saw the value. Wow, I sighed. Look at all the potential here.

We sat down and talked with the sellers, a husband and wife, and watched their boys and ours playing in the backyard. I moved into my professional sales woman role, and explained that I had started a new job a few months ago, and both of us were gainfully employed. I was upfront and honest about our credit history and produced my nine pages of ugly credit for them to review.

"Have you considered a lease option for selling this place?" I asked, hopefully.

The sellers looked at each other and the woman shrugged. The man said, "Not really, how does that work?"

"It's where we lease the house from you, and half of the payment goes toward the selling price of the house. It allows us to build a down payment to buy it, and allows you to keep the mortgage paid until we do," I explained.

We negotiated back and forth and the sellers agreed to have the house appraised. It came in at $205,000, so we settled on a lease-option-to-buy agreement, based on that appraised price. We agreed to pay three months' rent up front, and then with each payment thereafter, half would go toward the price of house. The lease was for 24 months, which would give us plenty of cash in the bank to obtain a conventional home loan.

We struck a deal and we thought we were the luckiest people in the world. We were close to Trevor's new school, close to Jesse and his other family, and had extra room for long term guests.

"We are putting down roots," I said to Michael as we began clearing the weeds and sprucing up the place. "I love this property." My new job at Pacific Bell was providing the stability of income we had lacked for so many years and every month our rent was paid on time. The boys enjoyed the rural atmosphere of our large lot, Trevor was doing great at his new school and Michael enrolled in Medical School. Our future was solid in our spacious new home.

That is, until about nine months later, when the seller of our house showed up at our front door.

He looked a little ragged, compared to our last meeting, but he wanted to pick up a baby grand piano that he had left with us, so I invited him in and offered him a cold drink.

I was not prepared for his words.

"I just wanted to stop by, and get the piano out of your way," he said. "But I also have to tell you something." After loading up the piano, he continued, "We moved to Idaho after we left this house, and my wife and I have split up. It's been a rough divorce."

"I'm so sorry," I told him sympathetically, but my sympathy turned to something entirely different when he continued.

"Well, there's more," the seller said, "I guess I should tell you that I haven't sent any of the money you've given me to bank. I haven't made any payments on the house either. So, foreclosure proceedings have begun on this house."

He turned away and shook his head. "Life happens, sorry." And he walked to his truck and drove away.

I was stunned beyond belief. All the money we thought we had accumulated toward a down payment on the house was gone. We were just beginning to rebound, feeling the footing of solid financial ground, and now to have thousands of dollars stolen from us was inconceivable.

The next day we came home to find our front door plastered with eviction notices. There were several notices, naming each of the occupants of the house, announcing that we had 30 days to move. It was humiliating and I was devastated. Michael was concerned and upset, but we tried to be strong for our boys. We went into our bedroom and prayed together.

"God, we are sure that you led us to this property," Michael prayed. "We would never have even found it but for you. It's perfect and we believe that you brought us here. Help us figure out what to do."

By this time in our marriage, we were so sure about who God was and confident in his power, both Michael and I trusted him with every fiber of our being.

Together with Michael I prayed, "God if you want us to be on the street and homeless we're ready. Whatever your will is, we are ready." Quietly, Michael and I sat in the bedroom and tried to listen for God.

My thoughtful, problem-solving husband stirred a bit and said, "I like the old saying, **'God can't steer a parked car'**; I think he wants us to take action…then He will direct us. So I think we should try to buy this house. Let's give it everything we've got. If it works, great. If not, then we'll just see where he leads us."

I was in total agreement with Michael's attitude and his trust in God. But with my real estate background, I knew that it was impossible for us to qualify for a home loan.

I got on the phone and called Valerie, my favorite lender, a patient, resourceful professional whom I trusted implicitly. I knew it couldn't hurt to try to get a loan, and if anybody could fund a risky buyer, Valerie could do it.

I went to Valerie's office and outlined what had just transpired with our lease option, how we had been making the payments just fine and our dream of owning the house. I explained that it was our deep desire to buy the house that was now in foreclosure. And then, for the first time ever of sharing my horrible credit history with anyone I knew professionally, I showed Valerie my vulnerability; all nine pages of it.

"I know getting a loan is a long shot. I suck on paper," I said as I handed over the nine pages and sighed.

"Well, let me see what I can do," Valerie said, as she took the file and I left her office.

That afternoon, Valerie started calling the creditors on our nine page credit report. I have no idea how or why, but one by one, each and every one agreed to remove their negative comments. Within a couple of weeks, all we had left was a $22,000 federal tax lien.

Valerie told us who to call to negotiate our federal tax lien, and within 10 days, the federal government agreed to allow us to pay $210 a month toward the taxes owed. If we started making payments immediately, they would remove their derogatory comment within 30 days. That meant that at the end of the next 30 days our credit report went from nine pages of ugly to one page of loanable credit!

Michael and I were amazed. This was a huge miracle. We were so grateful to God. We had gone from, "We're happy to live on the street if you want," to God cleaning our credit report which allowed us to buy a home. The problem wasn't solved yet, but we had hope.

The house had been appraised for $205,000 so Michael and I anticipated our loan would need to be that much. We were on the brink of discouragement, when Valerie informed us that with our clean credit, we now qualified for a $165,000 loan. That was an amazing miracle, considering what we started with, but it was still $40,000 short of our goal.

"Well, maybe we can find a house for $165,000," Michael said to me, looking for the silver lining in our situation. We were getting ready to meet with the banker who was handling the foreclosure. He had been so mean and disrespectful to us in the beginning, treating us as if we were the ones who had defaulted on the loan. I wasn't looking forward to another confrontation with him, but Michael and I went together to negotiate the details of when we had to vacate the property.

We walked into a conference room, and sat down across the table from the mean, surly banker. I started to say something, but as I opened my mouth the banker held up his hand like a stop sign and demanded, "Wait. Before you say a thing, we won't take a penny under $142,500."

I was stunned. It wasn't even $165,000!

Without saying a word, I pulled out our pre-approved loan letter and Michael and I bought the house for $142,500 on the spot. God not only gave us the house of our dreams; He gave it to us with $62,500 in equity.

It was another enormous miracle. Looking back I can see that God was not only concerned with where we lived; he was helping us clean up our mess. I believe He honored our growing faith and obedience to put Him above our own desires. And He blessed us with an incredible piece of prime real estate nestled in the Sacramento suburbs. After closing on the sale we set down deep roots, making improvements, upgrades and landscaping. Michael, a Midwestern boy who loves barns, designed and built my studio barn and then designed our hay barn, which is our outdoor living area, perfect for entertaining year-round in the Sacramento climate. We enjoy a lovely raised bed garden and thrive in the quiet peace that has settled over the property. As I walk from room to room and space to space on this property, I feel so blessed. It is 100 percent a gift from God.

Everything we have built on our lot we have given to God in prayer. We wrote scriptures and prayers on all the underpinning wood before we covered it with finish work. We have asked for God's blessing on every project. Our home is peaceful, inviting and we know the Holy Spirit lives here with us.

I spent so many years trying to create a facade of my life, trying to be what is considered acceptable in the American race for a perfect life. I look at everything in my past, and the lessons I learned, and I'm not ashamed of it anymore. I know that God has forgiven me for my myriad of mistakes and that he is faithful even in the midst of them. When people come to visit and ask about our home, unabashedly I tell them the story of how God gave it to us, and it always begins with nine pages of ugly credit and a faithful God.

13

BLINDSIDED

Even though Michael and I were making progress in our marriage, and enjoying an intimate relationship with God, we still had normal life challenges. Finances, finding satisfaction in our jobs, raising adolescent boys, normal life stuff, was still all around us. With God in the midst of it all, we managed with little conflict and relative peace. We were active in Bible study and stepped up to help others whenever we could. We felt confident that we heard God's voice when we prayed for guidance and we believed, no matter what, God was with us.

Michael was working at a health clinic when he met a woman named Claire who had a horrific past. Claire was Michael's supervisor and she made a point to be nasty to him when she learned he was a Christian. Nevertheless he continued to show her kindness. Over time she softened and we both reached out to Claire, who we learned was afraid of her family and had no one to care for her failing health. Claire told us how she had grown up in a satanic cult in Southern California with horrible stories of abuse. Her body was riddled with HIV she had acquired through tainted needles when she had been injected with hallucinogenic drugs. She was an outspoken atheist. With God's guidance, and a lot of patience, Michael and I showed love to her, invited her to church and after a couple of years she accepted Christ into her life.

Claire lived in Woodland, about 30 miles from our home. She had been spending a lot of time with our family and her edges were softening. Then she began receiving threats from her satanic cult family in Southern California. She told us about finding a threatening note attached to the collar of her dog. Claire was terrified that she was not safe in her own home.

Michael and I prayed together about Claire's situation and believed we heard God prompting us to invite her to move into our home. We had plenty of room, and we were so much closer to the church than where Claire was; it would be good for her on many levels. We talked with the boys about it, and they agreed that it would be a good idea. So we moved Claire, and her Golden Retriever, Brewster, into a guest room in our beautiful Carmichael home.

The boys loved her. Claire was playful with them and fit right into our lifestyle. My sister, my friends, even my mom loved her. Claire just merged into our family, hanging out with us, going to church with us, and helping around the house as much as her debilitated body would allow. Claire said she thought she was the luckiest woman in the world.

Claire's illness progressed. She would often wake up in the middle of the night, writhing in pain. She would take some morphine and then call out to me to come into her room and comfort her until she fell back asleep. Her HIV was now full-blown AIDs, she had developed cancer, which was spreading, and she needed a cane to walk due to painful neuropathy in her feet. Still, Claire became a youth leader at our church, and even went on several mission trips to faraway places. It was amazing to watch how she could press on in the midst of disease, disability and pain.

Claire had been living with us for eight years when my teenage son met a friend of a friend who had worked with Claire years ago. Claire's name came up innocently in conversation, until the friend asked some questions about Claire's last name, and other identifying details. Then he told my son, "Watch out for her. She's a pathological liar. We had to fire her at the group home where I worked, for a 'fabricated resume'. She claimed to have a degree and work experience that were completely false. Be careful."

Baffled, my son came home and shared that information with me. I couldn't believe it. The description just didn't line up with my paradigm. But I couldn't ignore my son's concern. "Let's ask Claire," I suggested.

Our family sat down with Claire for an explanation. "We are a little concerned and confused," I told her. "Do you know anything about these accusations?"

Claire listened carefully and then said, "Oh I'm so glad you asked me, because I definitely don't want you to be confused about that." She rattled off a plausible story that explained a miscommunication. "Please don't worry about it. And you can always come to me with any questions."

I felt so much better. I believed her version of the story and Michael and I let it go. We wanted to believe the very best of her. My son, however, had a sixth sense about it. He smelled a fish. And when I believed Claire's story and not my son's suspicions, it drove a wedge into our fragile parent/teen relationship.

Oddly enough, about two weeks later, a physician and his wife, who lived just two minutes from our church, invited Claire to live with them. Claire's pain was increasing, her disabilities more exaggerated and this family thought their location would help ease some of Claire's challenges in getting to her various jobs at the church. By now, in the final stages of AIDS, her cancer was worse and everything in her world was painful and hard.

"I appreciate all you guys have done for me," Claire said as she was packing up. "I've been invited to live with a family right next to the church. So I'm going to move."

Claire had been living with us for those eight years and we had come to love her as a member of our family. But caring for her many health complications and constant emotional neediness was exhausting. I was ready to share that load with another family. So we said good bye to Claire and wished her well. I knew that I would see her at church; she was always there, involved in one project or another.

Because of her childhood traumas, Claire had privacy and boundary issues. She kept all of her medications locked up in her bedroom. She was very private about taking them, so when she moved in with the physician, he respected this practice and had no concerns about how Claire managed her illnesses.

The pastor at the church however, had suspected something was amiss with Claire for a while. After she moved in with the new family, his crap detector waved a big flag. Claire never did anything on her own. She needed help with every aspect of her life, except for her doctor appointments. She always went to her medical appointments alone. I respected this as part of her boundary issues, but the pastor wasn't buying it.

One day the pastor had her followed to a doctor's appointment, to confirm his suspicions that she didn't have an appointment. Further investigation revealed that Claire was a clever, manipulative, prolific fraud.

The pastor called an intervention. He brought the church leaders who worked with Claire and the family where she now lived together and confronted her with the evidence. She admitted to the things they caught her with. She didn't have HIV, she didn't have AIDS and she didn't have cancer or neuropathy or any disability.

Michael and I were not invited to the intervention. I don't know why we were left out, but it hurt. Claire had lived with us for so long and we had been the most deceived by her treachery. The pastor called us and told us the truth. We were beyond shocked.

After that we met with the intervention group and the pastor, just to learn more about the depth of Claire's deception and lies. I was stunned to learn that Claire admitted that all of her illnesses and sad stories of abuse were a huge farce. She did not apologize for the deceit, and she only admitted to the specific parts that had been found out. At that point, the pastor laid out a plan to minister to Claire. He planned to bring her around to God's truth, and told us all that Claire was still going to be part of the church.

I was astonished. This woman had stolen from the church with her lies. We had fund-raised thousands of dollars to pay for a Make-a-Wish style Disneyworld trip for her. There was a big poster of Claire in the church that told her redemptive story. They took the poster down, but the congregation continued to minister to Claire. No one reached out to me or Michael, or our children.

There were so many emotions swirling in my head and my heart that I couldn't separate them. I felt angry, embarrassed, foolish and betrayed on so many levels. Shortly after that, Claire came by the house to apologize to us and allow us to ask questions. This was step one of the pastor's plan for redeeming Claire.

I tried to press for answers about so many things we had worked through, her medications in the middle of the night, the pain she claimed to own, the abuse by the satanic cult, her hair falling out from all the chemo. But Claire wouldn't give an answer to any of it.

"I've been lying about so much for so long that I don't know what is truth and what's not," Claire said.

With no resolution and no authentic remorse, I didn't want to see Claire again. I didn't want to run into her for a very long time. Her lies had caused untold damage to our family. If she was going to still be involved at church, I couldn't be there. My son Trevor was especially bitter and angry, feeling betrayed by God, and pushed himself as far away from church life as possible.

Why had God allowed this? The thought reverberated through our minds. Michael and I knew that God's promises were true. We had prayed in earnest before we even began to minister to Claire. We had prayed and listened for God's voice when we had invited Claire to live with us.

"Do we not know your voice?" I pleaded with God. "Why would you allow her to live with us for eight years, damage the faith of our sons, and wound our hearts, only to have it end this way?"

Neither Michael nor I believed that God had left us, but we did wonder if we weren't hearing God's voice. We pondered how do we know God's voice? How can we continue to minister, if we can't trust the direction we feel from God? For the next year, we stayed at home on Sunday mornings. We still prayed, we still read our Bibles, and we still continued to seek God's voice. But we were rocked in a huge way.

It took a year of licking our wounds, before we felt healed enough to come out of hiding. In the end, Michael and I decided that what we did for Claire was what we believed God would have done if he were here. We took someone who said she was broken, loved her like Jesus would, and we gave her everything we had. What God does with that now, we have to leave up to him. I know in my heart that our intent was pure with Claire. To allow Claire's deceit to keep us from serving others is not God's will.

The big question facing us was, "How can we continue to do ministry if we can't discern a massive fraud from a sincere God-seeking person?"

The answer we received was, "We can't."

All we can do is love God and love others. Michael and I decided that we had to keep loving others and trust that God would work out the details in the long run. With that resolution, we started looking for a new church near our home. God led us to one that we loved.

It took me a number of years before I could forgive Claire. Even now, as I think about those years, it is painful, but I sincerely hope God has turned our trial into something beautiful. I know for a fact He can do that.

14

CAREER CHALLENGES

Enrolling in the Dale Carnegie Course in Effective Speaking and Human Relations was a pivotal point in my life. Prior to that, I had been completely focused on trying to excel at everything I did and yet deep inside I felt like a fraud. Day after day I pretended to be the strong, capable, intelligent woman I wanted to be and yet it was just a mask I wore. To be honest, it was exhausting trying to convince myself and everyone around me that I was all that I wanted to be. I refused to be a victim. I'd grown up with sayings like, "Don't wallow in a pity party, pull yourselves up by the bootstraps and get on with life." And that is what I did.

At the time I inquired about the Dale Carnegie Course I was working for a company called Image Control Associates selling industrial photographic equipment and supplies. My position was Inside Sales but I really wanted the Outside Sales position, which covered the territory from Bakersfield to the Oregon border. Naturally I thought the Dale Carnegie Course in Sales was what I should take. But when I sat down with a representative and learned about the benefits of the various courses, I chose the Effective Speaking and Human Relations Course. With a money back guarantee, I committed to 14 weeks of classes. Not only did I learn to effectively and concisely communicate, I grew in confidence and compassion for others. It was where I started to believe that I had value. As my confidence grew, in conjunction with humility, I began to find my voice and defend myself against the lies I continued to hear from those in my life.

It made such an impact that I went on to be a group leader in future sessions. I also took the 12 week Dale Carnegie Sales Course and got the promotion I wanted to Outside Sales. I enjoyed selling commercial photographic equipment up and down the State of California. I had continued volunteering in the Dale Carnegie Courses and grew in my confidence and skill each time I served. It got to be comical after a while; I was spending so much time volunteering in the Dale Carnegie classes as a group leader that the franchise owner suggested I come to work with them. I loved the training and had watched not only myself benefit tremendously but time and again I would see life-changing results from everyone who really committed to the work. It was undeniable. Unlike a short term seminar, which studies show most people forget about within 3 weeks of taking, Dale Carnegie Training was different.

The courses were structured for behavioral changes to take place. We would meet once a week for 12 or 14 weeks (depending on the class), for 4 hours at a time. Each week we would introduce a topic or skill and practice it, in the safe environment of the classroom. Then participants would be charged with taking the newly developed skill back into their daily life and putting it into practice. If they had trouble during the week, they could reach out to their group leader for help. Week after week, participants would come back to the classroom and report on their experiences. New skills would be added and continuing the real-life practice was essential.

I knew it would be easy to sell the benefits of this training but it was not inexpensive. The classes, at that time, were around $700 each, which was a significant investment. We promised a money back guarantee at the end of any course if a person came to class each week, did the work and did not see tangible results. In all my years working with this organization I never had to return anyone's money.

The challenge was that it was a straight commission job and for each new enrollment, I only earned $100. The courses were great but the factor I couldn't control was the fear that people had. These courses required you to work hard and be vulnerable. They required you to try new things, knowing that not every time would be successful at the first try. The franchise owner knew his business well and advised me this was a numbers game. If I made 10 cold calls, I would get one appointment; if I saw 4 appointments, I would make one sale/enrollment and earn $100. That meant, that in order to earn $2000 a month (in 1984) I had to make 800 cold calls each month. Ewww!

The alternative was to speak to groups. The same numbers applied, so when I spoke to a group of 40 people, which took about an hour, I would average 4 appointments and make one sale. I also got referrals to other groups or individuals and quickly discovered this was the way to go.

I loved my new job at Dale Carnegie & Associates. It was hard work, long hours, and straight commission with no vacation or sick days and no retirement plan, but the intangible benefits were beyond value. Some of my greatest lessons learned came from time I spent with this organization.

Not long after I started speaking to groups, I began getting referrals to more and more people who worked for the local telephone company, Pacific Bell. One day I was introduced to a manager in one of the various groups within this huge organization and she asked me if I would speak to her team at an upcoming meeting. I offered talks on Stress Management, Time Management, Effective Communications, Customer Service, Controlling Worry and a number of other relevant topics. It was typically a 45 minute presentation, which included a brief summary of the Dale Carnegie offerings at the end. I asked for feedback on 3x5 cards, which is where I learned if a person was interested in hearing more about our classes. The last feedback question was always, "Is there anyone else you know who might benefit from a talk like this?" I always got at least two or three referrals.

As my business increased with Pacific Bell I started getting a familiar question from more and more employees, "Does Dale Carnegie Training qualify for Pacific Bell's Tuition Reimbursement Program?" I had no idea. Over the next several weeks I dug deep into this organization and was put in touch with the folks who managed that program. I found out what the requirements were for a course to be accepted and sought to fulfill those requirements. Within a few months, DCT tuition reimbursement was approved for any permanent Pacific Bell employee. This opened the world to me and over the next year I spent most of my time just doing talks for Pacific Bell and meeting with their employees. I was a top producer for Dale Carnegie with 75% of the Franchise's income coming from this one company, with no shortage of future business.

Along with selling the courses during the day, we were expected to attend or volunteer as a group leader on the evenings when classes were held. I was committed. I went through a rigorous boot-camp type training for trainers as I worked to become certified as a Dale Carnegie Instructor. It was the most challenging, expansive and fruitful training I've ever experienced. I was constantly stretched outside my comfort zone.

When Michael and I were blessed (and surprised) with our son, Trevor, I had been working full time for Dale Carnegie Training for nearly 4 years. Throughout my pregnancy and the years prior, I had developed such a close relationship with Pacific Bell that I had a vendor badge and inevitably ran into past students/participants everywhere I went at the Pacific Bell facilities. I felt at home with this customer and they seemed to equally appreciate what I had to offer. Some had asked me what I was going to do after the baby was born. What I really wanted to do was be a stay-at-home mom with my new baby for its first year of life, but I knew I had to continue to bring in some income.

Since Dale Carnegie Training was a straight commission job I decided to propose to the franchise owner that I work from home for the next year focused exclusively on the Pacific Bell account. I had grown this account from a handful of random enrollments to a consistent provider of full classes. I reasoned that I could have my mom stay with the baby when I gave talks and if necessary, most of my customers were okay with me bringing a sleeping baby to a coffee shop when we would meet to talk about the classes. I know it would have worked. But the Franchise owner wanted a 100% commitment. I could not be a mom and work for Dale Carnegie and Associates at the same time. He gave the Pacific Bell account to a brand new representative and said good bye to me.

It was heartbreaking. Another case of me putting my heart and soul out only to have it stepped on and twisted. Years later, the franchise owner met me and apologized for how he had handled the situation. It was sincere and I accepted his apology. I was happy for that resolution as I will always have the greatest respect for Dale Carnegie Training. Meanwhile, my beautiful baby boy was born and he made up for the disappointment of leaving the Dale Carnegie business.

Still needing to make money I registered a business license for McClanahan & Associates, a company that provided training in customer service and sales for property management companies. I would go to apartment complexes around town posing as an interested renter to evaluate their property. Based on a detailed scorecard that evaluated everything from curb appeal to first impressions, staff friendliness, apartment readiness and more, I would make notes and comments that I would later use to contact the owner or property manager to offer training.

I developed everything from logo to training materials and enjoyed enough success to get us through. Meanwhile I was still finishing my Bachelor's Degree and had recently decided to get my real estate sales license. Between my years with Dale Carnegie and the succeeding years in real estate and training, I was always self-employed. This meant that every time I earned a paycheck, I was paid the full amount, with nothing held back for taxes or social security. I also needed to be saving for medical expenses and unforeseen emergencies, but we never had more than just enough to survive.

In May of 1990, beneath unexpected rain showers I walked proudly across the outdoor stage at CSU, Sacramento to receive my bachelor's degree. My children, husband, in-laws and mom were wet witnesses. It had taken me 15 years, but I did it! I had started as a Business major because that's what other people thought I should do but instead I chose to become a Geography major. I knew I wasn't doing the typical, "Decide on a degree, go to school and get it, then get a job in that field," plan, so I wanted a degree in a field that I loved. Part of what kept me going for 15 years was the fact that I loved nearly every class I took. I loved meteorology and still enjoy searching the skies and the Doppler reports for what is coming. I loved cartography - the study of maps. I am a collector of maps and they have now begun to show up in my art. I loved physical geography - the study of flora and fauna; and I loved the study of cultural geography - why certain people groups ended up where they did and how their unique cultural practices evolved.

In the same year I opened a real estate office with a wonderful man, Jacob Daniels. He was a kind and generous man with a wealth of practical experience in the field of real estate. He was exceptionally creative and specialized in orchestrating two or three-way 1031 Tax-Deferred Exchanges for folks wanting to move their commercial properties.

The real estate market was difficult at the time and I loved learning new and creative ways to approach challenging situations. In time, I joined another firm that specialized in property management. With my earlier background in training they hired me to be in charge of bringing in new accounts to manage, as well as training staff for optimal results. The training resulted in higher occupancy rates with less turnover making properties more valuable to their owners. If they desired, we would also represent them in the sale or exchange of their property. It was a win-win. Marsha, the owner and broker oversaw the entire business and welcomed the skills I brought to the team.

By 1991, I was experiencing more and more fatigue and pain through my body. I had seen numerous doctors over the years but no one seemed to know what the problem was; they just kept giving me more pills to treat the various symptoms; narcotics for pain, sleep aids for night time, uppers for day time, anti-depressants for the ever present darkness and on and on.

I enjoyed the creativity of the real estate industry but by the time I left I was seriously burnt out. I had no boundaries. Interest rates were sky-high, which made it nearly impossible for many buyers to obtain financing. For every three or four escrows I would manage to open, I was lucky if one or two made it all the way through to closing. Financially we were hanging on by a thread back then, using all of our income to survive while accumulating those federal tax liens and a mountain of debt.

In 1993, after the affair, as Michael and I were working to breathe new life into our marriage, we moved to a new church. It was a spirit-filled, bible-based Episcopal Church and we loved it. One morning I received a phone call from a gal named Holly. I didn't really know her except that I had worked with her in children's ministry and knew her to be a devoted follower of Jesus. She told me that God had been waking her up at 2 a.m. each morning for the last three days with a message for me - and she wanted to get some sleep. She asked if I could please come over so she could deliver the message.

As I drove to Holly's house I couldn't help but think of the last time, during that healing service at Cursillo, when someone had delivered a "message from God" to me. It had opened

Pandora's Box, which led to some of the best and worst times of my life. I was more than a little bit nervous.

I sat down with Holly and she repeated what she had told me on the phone, then she went on to say, "I keep waking up with God telling my spirit to tell you, 'Stop worrying. Let go of the guilt. Trust me.'" She asked me if that made any sense. I was sure it would, but I needed some time to pray and listen.

I thanked Holly for her obedience, wished her good sleep in the nights ahead, and headed for home. As I sat with my journal and prayed for God to give me clarity regarding Holly's message, I remembered the bad mom label. For years I had been struggling to be a good wife, mother and provider, without sacrificing anything. The truth was, I took pretty good care of all my responsibilities except when it came to self-care. I hadn't even heard about that yet.

I continued praying and quietly, God began to show me my reality. I was working nearly around the clock trying to keep enough business in escrow to hopefully come out the other side and pay the bills. Every time the phone rang I was sure it would be another client who wanted to see EVERY house that might meet their needs, even though I knew the chance of qualifying was slim to none. I was exhausted. I had thought about getting a "real job," one with a steady paycheck and benefits, but I needed the freedom of self-employment to allow me to be available for my kids. I didn't want to miss a game or be away when they came home from school. It seemed I was once again between a rock and a hard place.

Then I thought of the message from Holly. "Stop worrying. Let go of the guilt. Trust me."

Stop worrying. Could that mean, "Stop worrying about being home for the kids after school"? or "Stop worrying about missing their practices and games"? or "Quit worrying about what other people will think"? What about the statement, "Let go of the guilt"? Could that mean, "Let go of the bad mom label"?

And then there was, "Trust me." That was the easiest and the hardest part. After seeing the miracles God was performing in my marriage, I knew I could trust him. But with my job? That was new territory.

As I prayed to God, asking him to reveal his meaning to me, I started thinking about Pacific Bell. I remembered when I was giving all the Dale Carnegie talks to PacBell employees that I had made a mental note: "If I ever wanted to give up being an Independent Contractor, PacBell would be a good company to work for." I had been in one workshop after another where I'd seen craft workers complaining about how bad they had it. Meanwhile I knew they were making twice as much money as I was and they had nights and weekends off. Plus full benefits! They didn't know how good they had it.

When Michael came home later I told him about my day. We talked and prayed together and I decided that it couldn't hurt to call Pacific Bell the next day and just inquire about possible openings.

As chance, or perhaps providence would have it, for the first time in 10 years Pacific Bell had opened a narrow window to the public for hiring residential service reps. Typically they had plenty of internal transfers and never needed to hire from the outside. I decided to apply. I was more than qualified and passed all their proficiency tests with ease.

Within two weeks I was offered a position by Pacific Bell. My prior sales, customer service and management experience allowed me to start at the highest level of weekly pay and that would automatically increase in six month intervals. There was medical and dental insurance that I desperately needed, a pension, 401K, vacation and sick leave. I thought I had struck gold.

Michael and I sat down with the boys and talked about the possible change. It would definitely be different around our house with me needing to be at work at 8 a.m. each day, but everyone was onboard. We decided to give it a try. When Jesse was with us, he could hang out with Trevor after school and when he wasn't around, Trevor could go to the after school program until I got off work.

Hanging on to the message Holly gave me, we decided to trust God. I quit worrying about what other people would think and tried to put away the guilt of being a bad mom. It was exciting to start a new adventure. I had been self-employed for so many years, just trying to make ends meet, this seemed like freedom.

On the other hand, I was tethered to a desk for eight-plus hours a day with one phone call after another being automatically routed to me as soon as I completed the prior call. At first I made a game out if it - how fast could I complete a call while meeting 100% of the stated requirements; how many calls could I finish in one hour? I started getting dirty looks from the other reps around me.

One gal took me under her wing and quietly explained, during a break, that the harder I worked, the worse it made the others look. I was stunned. It never occurred to me to work slower than I was capable. Having been self-employed for so long it was a matter of survival to work as hard and efficiently as I could if I was going to make a living. Here, however, we were paid the same whether we handled as many calls as possible or pretended to be on a call to trick the system into not sending more.

In those first few weeks I also noticed a number of processes that could be improved with minor tweaks. But when

I mentioned them to my manager I was basically told to shut up, sit down and do my job. Apparently I was making a lot of people look bad.

Within three months I had mastered my new job and found myself bored to death. I had been told during the interview process that I would not be eligible for promotion or transfer for 24 months. They knew I was overqualified for this position and wanted to be sure I would stay committed for two years before wanting to go elsewhere. Having never been in a position like this before, I optimistically said yes.

In the mornings before work, I cried out to God for help. I told Him I couldn't stand to be chained to this desk; surely He wanted more for me than this. But the more I prayed the more convinced I was that God was speaking to me. Essentially He told me the same thing my manager said, "Shut up, sit down and do your job."

But when He said it, it was different. Once convinced that the Creator of the Universe had told me what he wanted me to do, I could do it without question. Even though my faith walk still had a long way to go, I trusted God completely. The challenge was discerning his voice. Once I was sure I was hearing him clearly, I didn't hesitate. If I felt convinced that he wanted me to stand on one leg and hop around the office, I think I would have done it.

So with renewed commitment I went back to work and settled in. I decided to do my job to the very best of my ability regardless of how it made others look. I kept to myself and was routinely given greater challenges. I could see that through my obedience, God was blessing me with new opportunities.

One of those opportunities came when a new second level manager came into our office. She was one of the managers who had invited me to speak to her team when I was with Dale Carnegie Training. She asked me in to her office, wanting to know how it was that I was now working here at PacBell. We had a wonderful visit and she promised to keep me in mind for future promotions.

Sure enough, 10 months - not 24 - after I began working for Pacific Bell, I was promoted to management and sent to the Customer Retention Unit. I felt honored and blessed to have been promoted so far ahead of schedule.

I enjoyed the challenges of the new position but apparently my independent spirit ruffled feathers in that job as well. After working 10 more months, achieving top producer status and winning every award or sales contest they offered, I was called into my boss' office. I remember it distinctly - it was the day before Christmas.

My boss told me they had some serious concerns and I had a decision to make. I was shocked. What part of top performer did they have a problem with? But it wasn't that. I was an Instigator. I had the audacity to ask the administrative manager to order more file folders when I saw we were nearly out. And I instigated the decorating of our cubicles for the holidays. The bottom line was this: I could either stay in this job (shut up, sit down and do my job) and be put on probation, to be sure I stopped stirring up trouble; or I could go back to the non-management residential service rep position I had before. I had one week to decide.

I was devastated. I knew I didn't want to be tethered to a desk again but I felt so rejected by the new team that I didn't know how I could continue working there. During my prayer time, God reminded me of the Pac Bell second level manager I knew from my previous job. I gave her a call.

We sat down for coffee and she listened to my story. She knew my other manager and assured me that this issue was more about the insecurities of my manager and didn't really have anything to do with me. Nevertheless, I had a decision to make. Stay where I was and be put on a "program," which felt like sitting in the corner with a dunce cap; or take a step backwards.

But God had a plan and it was unfolding. The second level manager made a suggestion. "Come back to our department," she said, "and I will make sure you have all the time you need to look for another position in the company."

Wow. I couldn't have asked for a better solution. In January of 1997, I went back to my job as a residential service rep and began a job search. In less than 30 days I was offered a position in the prestigious "State of California Branch," where I became an Account Manager and was given a particularly challenging State customer to manage.

Little did I know what a coveted position I had been given. In no time at all I was issued a laptop, cell phone and home office equipment so I could telecommute part time. I spent most of my days seeing clients in downtown Sacramento and had the flexibility to work from home or the office between meetings. Instead of being threatened by my entrepreneurial attitude, I was embraced. I had a group of accounts and a quota to meet, or exceed, and I was left alone to make it happen.

Suddenly I could see what God had been doing. Nearly two years before, when Holly had shared the message God had given her, he had told me not to worry. Now I could see why. I was earning far more money than I had ever dreamed of and I had evenings and weekends to myself. We had a savings account that was quickly growing due to the company-matching program they offered. I found an amazing dentist who worked with me over several months, catching up on years without dental care and the list goes on and on. The best part though was the freedom. Since the new management gave me the flexibility to plan my own schedule, they didn't mind if I went to my sons' sports games or school programs. As long as I met the stated goals, I could do whatever I wanted.

In hindsight, God gave me ALL the freedom I had as a self-employed independent contractor but with the security of a steady paycheck and so much more. Every time I trusted him, he proved himself to be trustworthy. It didn't happen overnight but I knew I could count on him to have my best interests in mind. With each situation like that, my faith and obedience grew stronger, but I still had some growing and healing to do.

When I joined the State of California branch at Pacific Bell I found pride in my work. I loved the company and I enjoyed the people I worked with. We had solid leadership and a substantial team of subject matter experts, customer service managers, dedicated account managers and highly trained back office support. We were proud of the job we did supporting the communications, data and mobile networks for all of our State agencies. It was a challenging job with ever-increasing responsibilities but Pacific Bell did a great job of demonstrating their appreciation for our hard work.

I consistently felt like I was a valued employee, which drove me to fully immerse myself in learning everything I could about my portfolio of services and my customer's operations. I loved building relationships, both with internal teams and with my external customers. It was a fantastic job and I will always be grateful for what the job God provided gave to me and my family.

But it wasn't all roses.

I competed fiercely with other telecommunications companies for multi-million dollar state contracts. Nothing was easy working with the State, and procurements could easily take up to 36 months to come to fruition. I worked hard, building relationships at all levels of the State, pouring myself into everything I did. I won top awards for production and consistently received commendations from my customers.

As time went on and Pacific Bell was consumed by SBC, the feeling of "family" started to diminish. It became less about supporting our employees and more about increasing the bottom line. In late 2005, when SBC became AT&T, the stress had increased exponentially and taken its toll on me. For nearly 10 years, I had been in denial about a diagnosis of fibromyalgia and yet I couldn't function without prescribed narcotics for pain and others to keep me alert and focused. I felt like a walking pharmacy.

As I look back on those years before May, 2015 when I gloriously retired from AT&T, I can see that God allowed me to experience a good deal of stress, heartache, disappointment and pain, in order to get my attention. I can see now that with each episode of stress, God was encouraging me to let go and just do my very best. I didn't need to be a straight-A student all the time. Just doing my best was enough. When a huge State contract was canceled just months before completion, and I took it as a personal loss - a dagger straight through the heart - God showed me that I was giving too much. "Set your minds on things above, not on earthly things." Colossians 3:2

Time and again he kept lifting my chin, encouraging me to keep my eyes on Him, and more and more I discovered there was nothing better.

15

STRESS AND LIES

Gymnastics was a huge part of my life when I was a child. Whether it was a response to the chaos around me, or just my physical make up, I preferred to cartwheel my way around the world. I loved the exercise, the thrill of the tumbling and daredevil flips mixed with the artistry of dance. But when I was 14, it all came crashing to a halt at a gymnastic meet, when I tried a back flip on the balance beam and hit my back on the beam as I fell to the mat. The medical evaluation included a diagnosis of Spondylolisthesis. According to Wikipedia that is "the forward displacement of a vertebral bone in relation to the natural curve of the spine, most commonly occurring after a fracture". The Orthopedist told me it was a congenital problem whereby a bone was missing and replaced by a ligament. He said it would make my back weak and insisted that I stop all physical activity. This destroyed my dream of becoming an Olympic gymnast, and I was devastated.

I had not been allowed to enroll in any physical education classes all through high school, due to my condition. But once I got to college, I decided that I needed to move again, so I enrolled in three college PE classes. I knew I should ease myself into action, but my body was craving physical activity and I jumped right in. A couple of months into the semester my lower back froze up. I don't recall many details as the pain was so excruciating. I was hospitalized and treated with strong anti-inflammatories and pain killers. Once the inflammation went down and I could stand up straight again, they sent me home. My enthusiasm and eagerness to get back in shape set me back a full year.

It was a hard lesson. The truth was I didn't trust doctors. They were too black and white. All or nothing. My intuition insisted that 'simply not moving' could not possibly be in my best interest long-term. On the other hand I had a lot to learn about moderation.

A couple years later, after I walked out on my first marriage and moved in with H#2 my health remained fragile. It was incredibly frustrating as it tarnished the facade of invincibility I was working hard to create. Under the stress of relationships that were dissolving, forming, and in flux all around me, my low back gave out again. One day it just froze. I could hardly stand up and the pain was so intense that I collapsed. Suddenly I realized I was paralyzed from the waist down. It was terrifying.

I was rushed to the hospital where I was again examined and evaluated. The emergency room doctor dug deep to find the root of my pain. "Tell me about your health history," he said gently. "Has this happened before?"

"Just once a few years ago," I said through gritted teeth. "They gave me some anti-inflammatories and pain killers and it went away."

"Okay, we'll order your records, to look into that," the doctor said, making another note on the chart. "What about before then? Anything interesting in your health history?

"Any surgeries or hospitalizations I should know about?" The doctor prodded.

I thought for a moment. "I had frequent bouts of tonsillitis and when I was five I had a tonsillectomy. The same year I developed a hernia and was again hospitalized for surgery."

"I see," the doctor said, scribbling on his clipboard. "Are you on medication now? Do you regularly take meds? Tell me about drugs in your life, even over the counter drugs."

"I don't use drugs," I said emphatically. "But when I was a kid I suffered from allergies all the time. In elementary school I was allergic to grasses, trees and weeds; animal dander, though that never stopped me from having a cat or two," I replied with a shy guilty grin. "And I was allergic to dust and mold and mildew. In those days I was drugged up with antihistamines day and night just to keep my eyes from swelling shut and enable me to breathe. But with the help of allergy shots, I've developed an immunity to most of my allergies," I said. "I only take allergy pills a few days a year now, when the seasons change."

The doctor wrote down more notes, "Okay, we're going to admit you, run a few tests and see if we can get you comfortable," he said sympathetically. He eventually prescribed more powerful anti-inflammatories and the pain killer, Percocet. That did the trick. In fact it took my pain and my memory both away. For three weeks I completely lost track of reality. I remember a friend telling me we had talked on the phone for nearly an hour, just before I called her again to see how she was doing. I didn't remember either of those conversations.

A few years later, in 1980, I came down with spinal meningitis. I never knew either of my grandfathers, but I had been told that at least one of them died from meningitis. I just thought I had a really monstrous flu, but when I went in to the hospital and they noted my symptoms – high fever, severe, unrelenting headache, flu-like achiness all over and I couldn't touch my chin to my chest, they immediately whisked me into a private room. There I received my first spinal tap. I was told to lie on my side and pull my knees up tight to my chest, as in a fetal position. Then I was told to lie perfectly still while they inserted an enormous needle into the spaces between a couple of vertebrae in my spine, syphoning off some spinal fluid to run tests on. The pain of the spinal tap was as bad, if not worse, than the pain I was already experiencing.

There were signs of both viral and bacterial meningitis in that first tap, which immediately sent me into quarantine. Apparently bacterial meningitis is very scary stuff and often life threatening. I was treated with IV antibiotics and finally got some relief from a narcotic pain killer. Additional spinal taps were taken over the next few days until it finally came back clear of meningitis. As mysteriously as the meningitis showed up, it vanished one week later and I was released from the hospital.

The next episode of spinal meningitis came a year and a different husband later. Again I was hospitalized for about a week until the spinal tap proved clear. This was during a very dark relationship. I think, especially during that time, I had refined my adaptation skills so that I seemed quite well put to-gether and highly functional to the outside world, but on the inside I was in great turmoil. I was afraid and I felt trapped.

Looking back on my health issues, it's clear that stress had always been a trigger accompanying every health crisis I've experienced. My back had been fragile since the gymnastics accident. But as I faced the loss of my gymnastics dreams, even as a young teen, I was determined that nothing else about me would ever be considered fragile. I began to build a facade of success to the outside world and I was good at it too. In reality, I was accumulating and stuffing new and deeper episodes of shame, worry and guilt way down deep, unknowing that they would inevitably resurface later in my life.

I remained active through the years but by the time I started work at Pacific Bell I had been seen by countless doctors for chronic pain all over my body. My neck and shoulders ached deeply; I had pain in my back, hips and knees, in my arms and chest; it was unrelenting. Even my scalp hurt. My ability to sleep was intermittent at best; I was depressed and yet, I just kept smiling, putting one foot in front of the other.

Being tethered to a desk phone for eight-plus hours a day as a union-represented residential service rep didn't help my discomfort. Hours upon hours (overtime was always available and paid time and a half) of sitting and typing took its toll. I developed carpal tunnel syndrome in both wrists and visited numerous doctors and physical therapists to learn how to manage those symptoms.

As years passed and my overall pain continued to increase, I was finally diagnosed with Fibromyalgia. However, when the doctor gave me the diagnosis it was almost as if to say, "Well, you don't have lupus or rheumatoid arthritis and you don't have these other conditions, so we're going to call it Fibromyalgia." I remember feeling like he was just giving me a diagnosis, like granting a wish with the wave of his reflex hammer, to shut me up. His attitude made me feel that he was hoping I would stop bothering him with my pain, now that he had identified a source.

Instead, I asked him, "How do you treat that?"

He went on to tell me that there really wasn't a way to treat Fibromyalgia (in the early 90's) other than to manage the symptoms. That meant drugs. I was given narcotic pain killers that became less and less effective over time as I transitioned from Vicodin to Norco to OxyContin and finally Methadone, each with increasing dosages. Since I continued working full time I needed more drugs to keep me alert while driving and doing my job - Ritalin, Provigil and more.

Depression is a common symptom of Fibromyalgia and I had been plagued with it for many years. So we added a few anti-depressants to the mix. Then there was the inability to sleep, so I had sleeping pills. It was a miracle I ever managed to get anything done. Still, I limped along quite gracefully for several years.

In 2001, I suffered another episode of spinal meningitis. I was hospitalized on the day we were supposed to fly to Dallas to be with a dear friend who was dying from brain cancer. Heartbreaking. I had also just received my third consecutive, annual President's Club Award, but I was paying a high price for that recognition.

Nevertheless, I recovered from the meningitis and managed to keep my pharmacopeia going, until late 2003. "Coincidentally," this was the same time we found out Claire was a complete fraud. Her betrayal cut deep.

Add to that mix, the stress that was building at work. I'd taken on some very large and challenging projects and succeeded repeatedly, so the bar kept getting raised higher and higher. "No good deed goes unpunished," was the catch phrase at the office every time quotas were set. And while I continued to excel, I also lost a huge, multi-million dollar contract. Initially I had worked diligently to win the contract and then, when we were just a few months from completion, the customer pulled the plug. From a rational, detached perspective, they had a right. Development was behind and our deliverables were overdue. But from a people-pleaser-perfectionist's perspective, they might as well have kicked me in the gut. I took the loss personally. I had given too much of myself and the executive clients really didn't care. I had worked exclusively with that single account for 12 years, giving them everything I had. I was their advocate, their partner and a member of their team. I had my own ID and Security badge and spent more time at their office than my own. It felt as if I had been betrayed – again.

Late in 2003, the house of cards started crashing down, one more time. Hadn't I been through this already? How much more onion was there to peel back? The Fibromyalgia pain and fatigue became unmanageable. To simply get out of bed and make it to the living room or my home office down the hall was an event. Taking a shower required a huge expenditure of energy; and if I had to raise my arms above my head to wash my hair, I was exhausted for a couple of hours. The weight of my arms seemed impossible to lift.

Thankfully I was blessed in my career at AT&T with great managers who I sincerely believe cared more about my health than my production. They trusted me to work from home knowing my strong work ethic would enable me to complete the job, in my time. Even if it took all day and into the night, through fits and starts, I always got it done. However, no matter how hard I tried, I couldn't deny that I was getting worse. The constant pain and debilitating fatigue were no longer controllable with meds. I took naps often, sometimes for three to four hours at a time, because that was all I could do. I hated it. I hated myself for not being strong enough to fight it. It was the first time in my life where, deep in my soul, I knew a few weeks of rest was not enough to make this better. I felt hopeless.

Thankfully, a friend blessed me with a small newspaper advertisement about a doctor who was giving a lecture on how to recover from Fibromyalgia. I looked at the ad and thought, "It couldn't hurt." As I sat in the room that day I listened to the physician describe how he had taken a year off from his rheumatology practice to really study and research Fibromyalgia. What he had learned was that there were several factors in common with nearly all Fibromyalgia patients. Most had experienced some kind of physical or emotional trauma as a child. CHECK. Most had strong personality traits that forced them to take care of others before themselves. CHECK. Many had been surrounded by unhealthy, co-dependent relationships. CHECK. Most had perfectionist qualities and were exceptionally hard on themselves when they perceived that they weren't operating at full capacity. CHECK. CHECK. CHECK. And, most had experienced another episode of physical or emotional trauma later in their life, which triggered the onset of symptoms.

I thought this guy had been reading my mail. I sat up a little straighter and tuned in more closely. Somewhere buried beneath years of obediently following doctors' orders I knew there had to be more. I knew that emotional trauma caused stress and stress could easily turn into physical illness but I had never heard a doctor talk like this. He spoke further about how the lab work of fibro patients very often resembled closely the biochemistry of animals who were in hibernation. It was as if our bodies were trying to shut down to preserve themselves. Finally he spoke about his methods of treating Fibromyalgia, not just managing it with drugs. In fact, he made it clear that if anyone chose to start treatment with him, they would either have to get off narcotics or would have to get refills from another doctor. It was not his way. I respected that.

And so I got serious with the business of conquering Fibromyalgia. My new doctor worked with me weekly to "reset my body" to its original default settings. I monitored my body temperature, weight, fatigue and diet carefully each day. In just three weeks, I started reducing the 90mg daily dose of methadone I had been taking for pain relief. That was a miracle! I had been told by other doctors that with the amount of prescription narcotics I had taken through my life there was NO WAY I would EVER be able to be free of methadone.

Within a year, I was off nearly every one of the 27 drugs and supplements I was taking to manage my symptoms. Beyond that, I was coming back to life. I was waking up from hibernation. There were a lot of factors that contributed to my healing. Many had to do with resetting the biochemistry in my body but another factor that I consider to have been equally significant was the journey I began of emotional healing.

With the support of my management and the encouragement of three different doctors and a therapist, I left my job on a disability leave-of-absence for four months in 2004. I had been working hard to heal, but my efforts were neutralized or set back with the pressure at work. I needed time for healing, without expectations. It went against everything in my being to admit that I needed to take this time off, but I felt God quietly encouraging me to listen. And all those around me were saying, "Yes. Do this." And so I did.

My husband had designed a beautiful art studio ("the barn") for me, a place to be creative without leaving a mess on the dining room table for days. It's in the far corner of our big back yard and it's a sacred space to me. It was during this four month period where I sat at my desk, in my studio, drawing and writing and seeking God's face. This was one of the hardest periods of my life because there was nothing standing between me and the complete truth. I had the time, I had the place, I had a God who loves me and a husband who encouraged me. I just had to step in.

Each day sitting at my desk overlooking our beautiful property, I opened my notebook and poured out my heart to God. I asked Him what He wanted me to learn. I surrendered all of me, sincerely, and waited on Him. I journaled extensively, making lists of the messages that had been imprinted on my soul over time - since I was a child. I took time to reflect on each message, and then I asked God to tell me His truth about each statement.

In my soul I heard, *"You're not pretty enough"*, but God said, **"You're BEAUTIFUL!"** My wounded spirit insisted, *"It's all your fault"*, but God said, **"Others have played a part."** And then came, *"When you win, your sister loses"*, but God insisted, **"That was never your fault."** My inner critic chimed in, *"You're a massive failure,"* but God countered, **"You've been successful many times"**. And on and on we went...

"When you do well, other people suffer." No, God insisted, **"You can only control yourself."** *"You're a loser,"* my critic jeered but God said, **"To me, you're a WINNER."**

I searched back further and found more messages: *"You're a bad mom,"* but God reminded me, **"You're a LOVING mom."**

I had believed my critic when she said, "*You're selfish*." But God told me "**You're not selfish enough**".

As I thought about all my failures I was reminded, "*You'll never be successful*." But God told me, "**Your story is not over**." I found another message etched into my soul – "*You're a bad wife / daughter / sister / friend...*" and God said, "**You're human**." We went deeper... "*No one loves you*." This had always been my biggest fear. God said, "**I LOVE YOU**."

I thought about the dreams I'd had as a child when I had come to believe, "*BIG DREAMS are for other people*," but God said, "**I have big plans for you**."

I continued to sit, pray and write in my journal...

"*Sex equals love; love equals sex*"...I was such a mess! But God insisted, "**I will restore you**." "*Please others or suffer the consequences*." No. "**Please ME. I'll take care of the rest**." "*You're not valuable unless you're productive*." Not true. "**You're valuable because I made you**." "*Resting is not productive*." Wrong again... "**Sometimes resting is essential**." The messages were surfacing more and more... "*You're not creative or artistic*." But God told me, "**I've given you many creative gifts**."

I remembered deciding early on that, "*Showing anger is NEVER acceptable*." But God reminded me, "**I gave you emotions to feel**."

As a child I had learned, "*Marriage is about secrets and lies*," but God insisted, "**Marriage is sacred**."

And on and on we went...

Time and again, God's truth shattered the lies I had built my life upon. In those first few weeks I watched as God systematically took apart the facade I had created. He tore down my pride, he expelled my need to put others first, he showed me how my constant doing - even for His kingdom - was not what he was after. He just wanted me. He just wanted me to rest in Him. "Be still and know that I am God." Psalm 46:10a became my mantra.

Little by little, it felt as if God was dismantling my life. I could see it all around me, like broken pieces of a clay pot scattered around my feet. And then, as if to make sure I didn't try to pick up those pieces and work some magic with super glue, God effectively smashed each piece into dust; impossible to reconstruct, even by the most talented CSIs. Jeremiah 18:1-6 puts it this way (italics mine):

> "This is the word that came to Jeremiah from the Lord: ² 'Go down to the potter's house, and there I will give you my message.' ³ So I went down to the potter's house, and I saw him working at the wheel. ⁴ But the pot he was shaping from the clay was marred in his hands; *so the potter formed it into another pot, shaping it as seemed best to him.*
>
> Then the word of the Lord came to me. ⁶ He said, 'Can I not do with you as this potter does?' declares the Lord. 'Like clay in the hand of the potter, so are you in my hand."

And that is where he left me for several weeks. He assured me of his intimate presence and unconditional love. But what about my life? What about my job? What about my responsibilities? What about all those people who depend on me?

"None of that matters," the Spirit whispered.

And so we went further. With the help of a trusted therapist I started revisiting the earliest memories of when I started believing the lies and using the various negative behaviors as coping mechanisms.

Thinking back on one situation after another, God showed me that I shouldn't have been put in that position and therefore my response, while it was life-sustaining at the time, no longer served me. In fact, now, those same behaviors were destroying me. For example, as a child I survived by predicting the onset of a violent outburst and pre-empting it with a distraction or diversion. I spent all my time in a battle-ready defensive stance, seldom able to just relax. As an adult, staying in that 'always-on' posture is a huge stressor and cannot be sustained without health risks. I needed to learn new strategies for protecting myself.

With one such tool, I learned about the fractured parts of my being. Some call it "compartmentalization." It's a coping mechanism; a 'divide and conquer' process for separating thoughts that conflict with one another. It starts when we're young, developing some parts of our personality more strongly than others. We develop a set of 'primary selves' which make up the persona we show the world. And at the same time, for each of our *primary selves* there is an equal and opposite 'self' that we have forced deep and out of sight. Without these parts, we are out of balance. What I discovered is that God wants us to be integrated. He made all our parts and each one is important.

My persona, by the time I was in high school, was supported by a strong responsible part, a very ambitious pusher, an impressive pleaser, a determined perfectionist, and an outspoken inner critic. I also discovered a desperately disowned Little Girl, a Rebel and many other parts as well.

I believe our parts are developed to keep us safe and help us feel loved. When we feel threatened, or conversely if we experience something we really like, we want to either stay away from or repeat the behavior that led us there. So when I came to learn that I was safer if I could predict a situation and diffuse it before it blew up, then that was good. I learned to trust the intuitive part of me and it served me very well.

I have found tremendous healing in acknowledging these different "parts" of me and inviting them to teach me the things I have forgotten. Adapting a technique called "Voice Dialogue", I invite the Holy Spirit to be my Center...the wise counselor who knows all my parts and can help bring us back together. When journaling I set up a dialogue, first inviting the Holy Spirit to lead me, then asking the other parts to speak up as needed. Quietly I wait, pen in hand, to see who will show up. If I've been feeling anxious and can't seem to shake it I will ask, "Who's feeling anxious? Please share." Usually my Pusher shows up first to remind me of the 50 things I should be working on rather than writing a book or watching TV. I love the Pusher for so many things. She never stopped pushing me get a Bachelor's Degree even though it took more than a decade and she has pushed me outside my comfort zone more times than I care to recall. Always for my good. But now when she shows up I have to lovingly tell her she needs a vacation! With the peace and confidence of the Holy Spirit I tell her that she doesn't have to work so hard anymore. And the journaling continues...giving voice to the many parts I've neglected for decades. It has enabled me to express feelings and thoughts from my childhood through the voice of the little girl who was "put away" when I had to grow up quickly.

I was terrified when it came time to return to work. I was afraid I wouldn't have the strength to set the necessary boundaries to remain healthy in a work environment. I sought the counsel of a long-time friend and life coach. We worked for several weeks to discern what I should do next. I was still 11 years from qualifying for retirement and I was fairly certain I wouldn't last that long.

God's desire for me to write and share my story came up time and again, as did dreams of creating a community center for art and healing. But in the end, it seemed the best thing I could do was set clear boundaries and learn how to hold them as I went back to work. If I could really keep to 40 hours a week of work and not give away my heart and soul, I would have the time and energy to start writing and creating on the weekends.

With that goal in mind I developed a written 30-60-90 day plan for re-entry. I met with each of my teams at work and told them briefly what I had been through and that I had to make some changes. I told them I would no longer allow customers to set unrealistic expectations that set us up to fail before we ever got started. I committed to arriving at customer meetings 15 minutes early instead of flying in at the last second after squeezing in three other "urgent to-do's" before leaving the office. I told them I would give 100% for 8 hours a day, 5 days a week, and no more. I would tightly hold my after hours to myself and would not answer calls or emails until the next day.

My co-workers were great. Many commented how much they respected me for the inner work I was doing and the boundaries I was setting. Some wished they could do the same. And my closest customers were terrific too. After working straight commission for so long in my early years, I never took for granted that someone paid me just to show up every day. I took that privilege very seriously and did my best to gain the trust and satisfaction of my customers. I learned early in my sales career that if a sale doesn't honestly improve the circumstances of a customer, you shouldn't be wasting their time pitching it. I never tried to sell anyone something I didn't honestly believe would improve their operations. In doing so I made some dear friends, many who have remained to this day.

Others... not so much. As my earlier fears had suggested there were plenty of people who clearly didn't like the new Pamela as much as the old one. Gone was the woman who would bend over backwards at every impossible request. I was still professional and did as much as I could to solve my customer's problems, but I was no longer emotional and frantic about it. I was methodical, honest and practical. But some of them still wanted Superwoman. Little did they know she had been shattered into dust and was not coming back.

Less than a year later, in 2005, my husband put together a lovely birthday party with some close friends and family. I remember distinctly when he raised a glass of champagne in a toast, "To my beautiful wife. I thought I had lost her, but now she is back. Here's to you, honey!" It made me cry. God had brought me so far...so many miracles.

16

THE GIFT OF HEALING

I was on a great roll toward complete healing and I continued to seek opportunities to better understand my body and cooperate with it in the healing process. It was during this time that I met some dear practitioners, Andrew and Naomi Downey. They are licensed chiropractors, in Newcastle, California, but what they do is so much more. They are healers. They are sensitive to each patient they see and gently guided me, week after week, to get in touch with various parts of my body that were locked up tight from decades of accumulated stress. During my time with the Downey's I have experienced more long-lasting physical healing from chronic pain in my back, neck and shoulders, than I ever thought was possible.

After walking my own path for so much of my life, and seeing where that got me, I no longer went anywhere without God. He was with me in the car when I was driving; he went to work with me; he was with me when I journaled; he encouraged me to create art; he watched over me as I slept and he was waiting for me when I woke up each morning. It became the kind of intimate companionship I had always longed for. I was learning more and more about the Bible during this time and I hung on to verses like Jeremiah 29:11-13, which says, "'For I know the plans I have for you,' declares the Lord, 'plans to prosper you and not to harm you, plans to give you hope and a future. Then you will call on me and come and pray to me, and I will listen to you. You will seek me and find me when you seek me with all your heart.'" And that is what I did. I sought Him with all my heart. Everyday. Everywhere I went.

One day I was visiting Andrew at his office and as always we started with a brief check-in. "How are you doing?" Andrew asked, as I settled in on the treatment table.

I wondered, was there anything in particular Andrew needed to know? I told him that I was doing pretty well but had this ever-present nagging pain deep in my back, between my shoulder blades.

Andrew asked, "Describe the pain. Think of it as something tangible. What does it look like? What does it feel like? Give me some details."

As I considered the questions, the answers came quickly. I took a deep breath. "It feels like a small bowling ball or maybe a shot-put. It's large, round, dark and completely dense."

Andrew nodded, encouraging me to go on.

I continued, "It's hard, completely impenetrable."

Andrew looked at me thoughtfully, "How long has it been there?"

I stumbled on that questioned. "It seems like it's always been there."

With that, Andrew had me lay face down on the table. Gently he lifted my ankles, as if checking the alignment of my spine as he viewed it from my feet. Then he proceeded to move about the table, touching me softly where he wanted me to focus breath in a particular area.

This was our usual routine and I always felt more spaciousness in my body after a session. But this day was different. While Andrew was going about his business, I had an incredible experience.

In the past, whenever I relaxed on the Downey's table, with my face pressed through the oblong hole, even when my eyes were shut, I could still sense the ambient light in the room around me. This time however, it was pitch black. I'm sure if I had opened my eyes and put my hand in front of my face I would not have seen it. Complete darkness surrounded me.

With Andrew moving about his work I was suddenly transported to the bottom of an ocean. It was impossibly dark but there were tinges of chroma, deep indigo and a dark, murky marine green. It felt as if I were an underwater observer – yet dry and able to breathe normally. As my eyes adjusted I could see a large, ominous creature on the ocean floor. It looked like a menacing shark, frightening me. Our eyes locked, and slowly it started ascending the depths of the ocean. As the creature moved higher in the water, I moved with it and the color of the water lightened into a deep turquoise. The water became so inviting, crystal clear, aquamarine and just as the creature broke the surface I realized that it had transformed into ME, a little girl about 8 years old with long flowing blonde curls and a peaceful smile. She rose out of the water and rolled onto her back where my younger self gently floated, contented face to the sky.

Wow. What was that? It reminded me of some wild trips I had taken in my rebellious years with the help of psychedelic mushrooms, but this time there was none of that. I was so startled by the clarity of the vision I couldn't even mention it to Andrew.

Pressing his hands against my back, Andrew said, "We're all done for now." I climbed off the table, gave him a hug and went straight to my car.

The most amazing part? The bowling ball/shot put was gone.

It took me a few weeks before I had the courage to talk to Andrew about what I experienced. As I tried to discern what the vision was all about, it became clear that I had experienced a supernatural encounter. After processing for a while, I discerned that the "creature" was fear and pain and it had manifested as an impenetrable shot put ball in the middle of my back. It was big and scary and had been with me for as long as I could remember. But now I was healing. God was showing me that it was okay to release that creature; it was okay to release that pain and fear, which had been bound so tightly for so many years that it seemed impenetrable.

With Andrew's help and God's encouragement, I was able to release the pain and free the little girl who lived inside me, to liberate that little girl who existed before the pain had begun to accumulate. It was another miracle. I still get aches and pains from time to time like most people my age, but that bowling ball has never returned.

The next ten years were a roller coaster ride. There were many amazing times, like when we took Trevor and a friend on a 10 day surfing adventure in Costa Rica; or when I first went to Kenya on a mission trip - and found my heart there. We celebrated family and friends, planted deep roots in our beloved Christ Community Church and continued to grow in our marriage. Michael's and my commitment to keep communication open and clear was determined. It wasn't always easy but we would not let the devil have a foothold. Regardless of circumstances, we stayed engaged in the process of learning to understand and love one another - no matter what. In fact, for the most part, my life was pretty awesome. I was blessed with three grandchildren and two daughters-in-law.

There was just one thing that wasn't working and it was my job. Once I returned to work after the disability in 2004, I noticed the spark that had once motivated me to push hard and exceed expectations was no longer there. I had once been motivated by sales contests and enticing trips to exotic places but now God had showed me that I didn't have to perform to be loved. I just had to be.

Every day I tried to remember Colossians 3:23 "Whatever you do, work at it with all your heart, as working for the Lord, not for human masters." And so I brought my bright spark into the office each day and gave it my best. But deep inside, I felt like a fraud. The truth was I didn't want to be there anymore. I had no passion left for the telecommunications industry. My patience waned as I had to deal with the immense bureaucracies of AT&T and my customer, the State of California. Every day I forced myself to get up and go to work. I counted my blessings and even printed them up and posted them in my cubicle so I would be reminded.

My health is restored.

My marriage is healthy.

We have a beautiful family, great friends and a thriving church.

I love my husband and he loves me.

I enjoy working with many wonderful customers.

I am blessed with a great team and supportive managers.

My income allows us to support a great many important causes.

It also allows us to take wonderful vacations and spend time with loved ones.

It also allows us to continue building out the property, which God gave us.

I have a pension and a 401K, which is accumulating every day that I show up.

And so on.

Still, the recurring rounds of forced-reductions were taking a toll on our business. Support staff and essential technical resources were being cut back time and time again; each round adding their responsibilities to our plate.

The weight got heavier and heavier. And after returning from my first mission trip to Kenya, it was even harder. I had experienced the best kind of work I could hope for... to love on people who had been thrown away by society. To tell them, "I came halfway around the world to let you know that you are not forgotten. You are valuable and you are loved." The deep joy I saw in those dear men and women who were suffering from AIDs was penetrating. It was all I could think about. My work at AT&T seemed meaningless. Irrelevant. As the struggle became harder I cried out to God, nearly every day, trying to understand why he was leaving me in such a stifling environment.

One autumn day, in 2011, I was driving up to see my chiropractor Andrew for another treatment. I had learned much over my years with Andrew and Naomi but as the stress at work increased so did my need for their continued guidance to keep my body open and connected.

As I drove, I was literally screaming at God, out loud in the car. "I can't stand it anymore. If I have to participate in one more billing meeting I might just go postal!" I was frantic. "God, I know you've blessed me with gifts and passion but it feels like they are being wasted at AT&T. Am I just hanging on to my job for the pension and retirement? Does that really mean I'm not trusting you like I should? Should I just quit my job, pull out my 401K and live on it while I build another business doing what I am passionate about? PLEASE, speak to me!" I was desperate for a word from God.

After my 30 minute drive, I arrived at Naomi and Andrew's 20 acre piece of heaven. The drive up and onto their property was as much a part of my treatment as what happened on the table. It is a magnificent piece of land covered with fig and other fruit trees, grape vines, and a beautiful multi-level pond large enough to paddle around with a kayak, all nestled amongst majestic conifers and mature deciduous trees, some already teasing with a hint of their fall colors. It feels like what I imagine when I think of Psalm 23... *The Lord is my Shepherd, I shall not want. He makes me lie down in green pastures. He leads me beside quiet waters. He restores my soul...*

I walked in to the office and checked-in with Andrew. "Anything I should know?" he asked.

"Just the usual," was my response. "My job is driving me mad. I honestly don't know if I can make it another four years to retirement." And with that I went face down on the table.

Andrew went through his usual method of assessing and treating while I had an incomprehensible encounter with God. My conversation had resumed, from the car, as soon as I was face down on the table. Still praying, I was pleading with God to speak to me, to give me hope, to show me how to survive the next four years.

All of a sudden, everything went pitch black again. Even with my eyes closed I sensed a deep but luminescent red source in the shape of a face - but without a face - just beneath the exam table. It was Him. He spoke to my spirit in a kind but direct manner.

God began, "OK, you're going to be doing public speaking. You will write books that share parts of your story and when you speak you will be able to expand or contract those chapters to fit the needs of your audience. You will continue to work at AT&T while preparing for this new vocation. You will keep strong boundaries, so as not to diminish your health. By doing that you will have energy and desire to begin this work of writing your story and telling your story. And by doing that work, you will be filled up enough to make it through whatever you have to face at AT&T."

BOOM! It was SO clear; it was scary. There was no ambiguity. This was the plan.

So I asked him, in my spirit, "I haven't done public speaking for 25 years. Why the hiatus?"

It felt like he smiled as he said, "Now you have something worthwhile to talk about."

Right then, Andrew's firm touch along my spine brought me back to the present as Andrew said, "We're all done for now."

I left the office, with a suspicious smile on my face. This was too good to be true. When I first started public speaking it was terrifying and I had a few tough audiences. But over time I became confident with my communication skills and found that I really loved sharing relevant stories with groups. I was so excited.

I spent the next half hour, driving home and continuing the conversation with God in the car. I wanted details. What topics should I write and speak about? Where do I begin?

God replied with this: "Answer the question, 'Why?' Why do you believe in me? What was life like before? What changed? Tell the truth."

It always amazes me that the Creator of the Universe would care so much as to desire a personal relationship with me. In Isaiah 55:8-9, God tells us that his ways are not our ways and his thoughts are not our thoughts. He says that his ways and his thoughts are higher than ours are. Therefore, I cannot presume to understand everything. I just can't because I don't think like God. All I know is that His ways are better.

When I arrived at home, Michael was still at work so I immediately grabbed my pen and journal and ran out back to sit on the swing and write. I needed to capture all that had happened and the plans I believed God had laid out for me. Much later that evening I gathered my courage to tell Michael what had happened. It was so overwhelming I was almost afraid to say it out loud for fear it would instantly vanish as quickly as it appeared. But that didn't happen. Michael shared in my guarded optimism. We prayed that, if this really was a word from God, that he would affirm it in the days and weeks ahead.

As if perfectly on cue, I had numerous "coincidences" over the next few weeks, one of which was being asked to speak to a Rotary Club in Rancho Cordova. With each 'coincidence' my gifts and passion were affirmed. Interestingly, the first group I ever spoke to was a Rotary Club in Rancho Cordova, 25 years earlier.

I felt God saying, "See, I'm bringing you back to where you began your public speaking career. This is just a warm-up."

I had to smile. I felt confident, though honestly terrified, that I had heard clearly from God. I knew it was my destiny to again speak before audiences, on topics from my life story, with lessons I had learned through my walk with and without God. This wasn't the first time I had had a vision of doing public speaking but by hearing it the way I did it came at just the right moment to remind me and give me hope.

17

BEING A MOM

I couldn't imagine writing a book about my life without including my children. There are tender memories that I treasure... moments of pure joy that still warm my heart. And there have also been moments, sometimes years, of heartbreak. To fully tell my story would require telling parts of their stories and those are not mine to tell. Suffice it to say that in both cases I loved every part of being pregnant, giving birth and raising my boys. I have learned a lot and I know I wasn't perfect. Far from it. But I know I did the very best I could with the resources I had. I have loved my children with all my heart and I will love them every day of my life.

My role model for being a mother was abusive, unstable, narcissistic and volatile. This was my "normal," and while I knew that not all mothers screamed and threw things to get attention, that was my reality. When I became a mother, I was determined to be kind, loving, unselfish, dependable, rational, and predictable; everything my own mother was not. My goal was to be a good mom.

When I ended the marriage to my first son's father, the judge awarded full custody to my ex-husband. The judge reasoned that since I worked full time, and my ex did not, he was more available and therefore a better choice than me. Essentially, the judge slapped a bad mom label on me. I was heartsick and grieved the loss of my son for many years. Eventually his father and I agreed on a joint custody arrangement, but the cloak of shame was always there.

I made mistakes as a mother, just like all moms do, but I always tried to do the best I could for my boys. I dodged that "Bad Mom" label in countless ways. I struggled for years to figure out how to balance being a mom and a provider. I thought I had to do it all. I remember feeling torn by having to put my son in preschool when he was just 13 months old. I had loved and treasured that first year with him and most of the moms I knew had gone back to work just weeks after giving birth.

Then, the year before Jesse was to start kindergarten his father suggested that we lighten the pre-school year to a three day week. This would give my little boy time to bond with his new baby sister, and it wouldn't interfere with my work schedule because he would be at home with his step-mom. I knew it was the right thing to do for my son, but it still hurt. Subconsciously it seemed to magnify the message that I was a bad mom. I just missed Jesse so terribly and in the back of my mind I kept thinking that if I could just figure out how to be a better mom, perhaps I would get my son back.

As the boys grew up, I talked to God about them all the time, and prayed for divine wisdom as their mother.

One memory still makes me smile. One night when Jesse was about four, I tucked him into bed and suggested that we say a prayer before going to sleep. I led us in a simple prayer and said, "Amen."

But instead of saying, "Amen," Jesse went right on to say, "Dear God, thank you for this day, but next time will you please make our heads out of rubber? Thank you, Amen."

After my irreverent past I was a little sensitive about joking with God. I tried to gently explain that God was real and it wasn't something to joke about.

My little toe-head looked straight into my eyes and said, "Mommy, I wasn't kidding. My head really hurts when I hit it on things and if it was rubber, it wouldn't."

This was the same child who loved to sing at the top of his lungs. One of his favorite songs was by Diana Ross, "Stop! In the Name of Love." Except Jesse thought the words were, "Stop! In the neighborhood!" I still change the words to that song anytime I hear it.

Jesse and I shared a love of music and art. He played guitar and was part of a band in his 20's. We also shared a love of nature. Some of my most treasured memories are from a trip Jesse and I took to the San Juan Islands off the coast of Washington state. We loved the outdoors and together we explored the island on scooters. I'll never forget the time we went kayaking. As we turned into a cove our guide invited us to stop paddling. "Let's just sit here a minute," the guide said, pointing toward a massive nest in the top of the trees along the shore.

Spellbound, Jesse and I watched as a mating pair of bald eagles swooped down into that enormous nest. Privileged to share this intimate glimpse into the lives of these magnificent raptors, we watched as they preened one another, cleaning their fluffy feathers and just doing life as we sat there on the water. It was magnificent.

Jesse grew up to become a skilled and talented finish carpenter and woodworking craftsman. Because he is so devoted to his wife and my two beautiful grandchildren, Jesse decided that he needed more stability in his career to provide for his family. After thorough consideration, he enlisted with the United States Military. Jesse has continued to excel in his field, earning commendations and promotions regularly. I am very proud of Jesse's dedicated service and his chosen career.

My second son, Trevor, has always been a bright spark in my life. From the very beginning, Trevor was an amazing gift to Michael and me, bursting with curious energy, an adventurous spirit and full of fun. His brother Jesse was in the room (with his own childbirth coach) when Trevor was born, and even though there were eight years between them, they developed a precious inseparable bond.

While Jesse was a mellow happy kid, and a doting big brother, Trevor was pushing the envelope from his first breath. As a toddler he was a dare devil, an explorer, and a wrestler, constantly keeping us on our toes. He was so full of energy, and ready to use it. I remember when he was just over a year old, playing at my feet in the kitchen and 15 seconds later he had power-crawled to the top of the stairs in our town house laughing down from the landing, where he could have easily fallen through.

Trevor brought a goofy kind of joy to our family, which included a daring sense of adventure. Once he started crawling, he was rarely without his favorite toy, a full-sized rubber mallet, in his little fist. He'd scoot across the floor, whack something, (like his big brother) and then move on to attack something else with the sturdy tool. Michael called him "Bam Bam." With Trevor's thick head of curly white locks and piercing blue eyes lined with impossibly long, curled lashes, he was often embarrassed by endless compliments.

As a child Trevor was smart and funny and always made us laugh. He developed an early love for computers, and at two years old he figured out how to use the old DOS operating system with a couple of Fisher Price computer games. One was a school bus, and by pushing the arrow keys he would guide the bus around the neighborhood to pick up the children for school. He had a similar game that was a fire truck that put out fires and saved kittens that were stuck high in the trees. At two he was amazingly proficient with the games and challenged himself to use the timers and complete all the tasks. Trevor was a straight A student in elementary school and enrolled in a rapid learner program. He seemed to enjoy everything. I loved watching him learn, chaperoning field trips and volunteering in his classroom. He was always happy, full of life and wonder. He was so curious, wanting to explore everywhere he went. Trevor made friends easily and had lots of them. He played soccer for years, and Michael and I were always there to cheer him on.

But the transition from elementary school to middle school was difficult for Trevor. He had attended our neighborhood school with the same 32 classmates since second grade, where he was honored and respected for his curious mind and serious work ethic. But when he left that learning environment to attend a school with 900 students, Trevor found out quickly it wasn't cool to be smart anymore.

The teen years were challenging, and prayer became my constant companion. And if one of the boys was in trouble, somewhere in the back of my mind, a voice would remind me that it was probably my fault for being a bad mom. Even in the pain of chronic illness, when parenting challenges arose, I would mentally admonish myself for not being strong enough, well enough, tough enough, good enough or anything enough to have prevented the current circumstance.

But regardless of my insecurities about motherhood, one thing remained constant; my love for my boys was ever present. I prayed for them daily and only wanted the very best for them. I recognized wonderful qualities in each of my boys as they were growing up and treasured the time I spent with them. God blessed each one with many talents, an abundance of compassion and a bright mind. Despite being what I perceived as a bad mom, my heart would swell with pride whenever I contemplated their success.

In 2004, when my boys were grown and off on their own adventures, I faced a health crisis that God used to open my eyes to a lot of things. One of them was the realization that I had been wearing the bad mom label for too many years. As with any old wound, this Bad Mom label left some brutal battle scars. Over a period of several weeks, through journaling and prayer, God scraped away the detritus - lies and pain from so many years of striving to be enough. I sought God's truth and he broke down my pride. He laid me out bare and I chose to look deep into all the open wounds. I discovered that I was not a bad mom, I was just a mom, flawed, but forgiven, damaged, but restored; and that was enough. That was enough for my boys and for God.

Recognizing that I was not a bad mother all those years didn't make everything instantly wonderful. Having a strong relationship with God didn't prevent damage to the relationships with my sons. Despite my deep, abiding love for my boys, we have endured heartache and hurt through miscommunication and loss of trust. Each day I pray, "Please bless my children; protect them and draw them close to you." I refuse to revisit the past of 'what ifs' and 'could haves'. Instead, I choose to focus on today and how God loves them more than I can even imagine. So I hold them close in my heart and I leave them in His promises.

I love looking at the pictures from when Trevor was a two year old budding computer genius. He proudly hangs on to those memories, knowing that he was meant to have a technology career from birth. Today Trevor has a degree in Digital Entertainment and Video Game Design, with several technology certifications he's earned, and enjoys a career in Information Technology Network Support with the State of California.

I have watched Trevor suffer through hurt and betrayal, and abandon all of his traditional goals for a 'live for today' attitude. The ache in my heart for his pain is matched only by the joy he brings. Trevor's smile, his zest for life and his daring adventurous nature encourage me and make me laugh. I am forever grateful for his presence in my life. His hugs are the best. His smile lights up a room. Trevor is a source of joy wherever he goes.

Meanwhile...at the time of this writing, I have been estranged from Jesse for several years. I cherish the memories of times together with him and I will always be grateful to God for my son. Sadly, Jesse and I have suffered a tragic pile-up of miscommunication, misunderstanding and conflict that has separated him from our family and broken my heart.

Being out of communication with my son is the deepest heartache I've experienced and the waves of grief wash over me when I least expect them. I just keep asking God to watch

over him, open doors for him and guide his path. And I pray
that God will fill this massive hole in my heart with his glory.
I would never choose this pain, nor wish it on anyone else. At
the same time, I know God's hand is at work.

> "'For my thoughts are not your thoughts, nei-
> ther are your ways my ways,' declares the Lord.
> 'As the heavens are higher than the earth, so
> are my ways higher than your ways and my
> thoughts than your thoughts.'" Isaiah 55:8-9

I keep a daily journal, and often my writings are prayers that
focus on my deepest longing, to be reconciled with Jesse and
his beautiful family. In my journal I also find refuge in sharing my thoughts, hopes, and dreams with my grandchildren
who are growing up without knowing me. Those precious
grandchildren are always on my mind and in my heart.

When I allow myself to think about being out of communication with my grown-up first-born, my emotions are raw
and vacillate between hurt, anger and deep dark sadness.
Depression can easily swallow me whole, if I linger too long.

I find myself taking a step back and rather than railing at
God to fix it, I ask him to show me what I can learn from the
tragedy that envelopes my heart. I trust that God is there in
the midst of it all and I rest in the comfort of His timing. As
much as my heart is shattered, I know God is with me. I have
prayed endlessly for resolution and I trust that He will answer
in His perfect time. Meanwhile I rest in the faith and confidence I have in the One who is always with me and will never
let me go. One day. Some day. I pray.

18

MY RICO

Just like I couldn't tell my story without mentioning my boys, this journey would not be complete without a chapter about my husband.

My dear Husband #4 - "Rico." His name is really Michael but as I was writing this book and we were talking about changing the names of some of the people in my story, Michael told me he wanted his pseudo name to be Rico! That's just a sample of his quirky Midwestern sense of humor. For years I didn't get it and I didn't think it was very funny but now it's among the many things I treasure about my sweetheart.

When I met Rico, the last thing I wanted was another husband. I was not praying for Prince Charming Number Four, and it didn't occur to me to ask God to put a good man in my life. I was just done. But Rico appeared on the scene first as a client and then as a friend. He was so handsome! But also genuine, relaxed, comfortable in his own skin, and he didn't try to impress anyone – especially me. Our relationship began so light hearted and Rico was so easy to be around that all my defenses collapsed and I began to simply enjoy him. It wasn't until Rico was set to meet my young son that I began to pray about our friendship.

When we first met, Rico was working as a stock broker for EF Hutton and Company. It was a seemingly prestigious job but the stress was high and he always had an economy-sized bottle of antacids nearby. You see, Rico is a kind man. He has a big heart. When older people would come in with their life savings and ask Rico to manage it, he would do so as if it were his own money. Conservative by nature, this meant Rico was not churning accounts. If a fund was supporting the needs of his client, he saw no reason to move their money or buy and sell other products. While this was good for the client it meant EF Hutton wasn't making as much money as they could have. Just before we were married, Rico was told he either had to increase his production or he would lose his job.

And sure enough, just after we married, he was fired. It didn't worry me because I thought Rico was an awesome stock broker. EF Hutton wanted him to churn vulnerable investors and he wouldn't risk it. I had huge respect for Rico for that. He rebounded quickly taking a job with a new start-up company that seemed to hold a lot of promise. Sadly, within 3 months they went belly up. It was a tough time for a lot of people.

For years Rico went through periods of unemployment or underemployment. I remember one of the lowest times in our life together when, out of desperation, he took a job selling chemicals designed to remove the grease from garage floors in auto shops. He loathed the job and left it after just 3 weeks. I was so angry and instead of understanding how dented my husband's ego was I began to feel resentful. I had been working my tail off from the time I was 14, doing whatever it took to provide for everyone around me, and I expected the same of him. I knew deep down in my heart that I shouldn't judge him, but in my self-righteousness I did. I was way more invested in how his unemployment affected me than I was about how it affected him and I'm sure Rico felt my judgement.

One day we received a phone call from a sister-in-law who knew of a job opening in a residential clinic for people who suffered brain trauma. It was a basic job - bottom rung on the ladder - helping patients with head injuries relearn the basic skills of daily living. Rico reasoned that at least it would get him out of the house and give him something to do. Little did he know this was all part of God's plan. While working at the clinic Rico met a nurse and a doctor, both of whom recognized his passion for helping others.

I could see changes in Rico as well. He now came home and wanted to talk about the patients. He was fascinated by the process of brain trauma and how it manifested behavior. I saw a passion in Rico that I hadn't seen for years. I was excited for him and very optimistic about his potential in this field.

It wasn't long before Rico remembered that he had begun his college career as a Pre-Med student, 25 years earlier, but had set it aside for a business degree. With the help of the doctor, he began to explore options and decided to pursue a midlife career change, which meant going to medical school. He was in his late-30's, which to most seemed too late to begin a daunting educational pursuit. But Rico's Midwestern grit propelled him into a whole new career path.

As a young boy, Rico had been put down by an influential first grade teacher who told him he couldn't spell and would never be any good at anything. That teacher was still in his head as he enrolled in our local junior college to get some necessary prerequisites out of the way. He fought hard to silence the voice in his head that told him he couldn't do it and with God firmly guiding his path, Rico got straight A's in Microbiology, Anatomy and Physiology and pretty much every other class he undertook.

As Rico's interest turned into a dedicated commitment to a new career, my attitude completely changed as well. I helped him every way I could. If there was anything I could do, I was available to support him. Right from the start of that commitment, I realized that Rico was destined to be a doctor, because no one could read his handwriting. But I learned to read his "chicken scratch" so I could type all of his papers for him. Each day I prayed for him as he studied, watching his passion for healing build.

The doctor from the head trauma clinic encouraged Rico to look into becoming a Physician Assistant (PA). It required the same pre-requisite courses Rico had already completed, along with two intense years of training, lots of clinical hours and would put Rico into the field as a health care provider working under another physician's license.

Rico's PA plan was formed and he continued to complete the necessary course work. While taking the pre-reqs, Rico was also volunteering his time at local health clinics in Sacramento to accumulate the clinical hours necessary before applying to medical school. After several years at the head trauma clinic and doing all the extracurricular work, Rico was ready to apply for the PA program at the University of California, Davis. Not only was UC Davis considered to be one of the top schools in the nation for medical training, it was located within easy driving distance of our home.

I was so proud of the direction Rico was headed and his dogged determination to be successful. God had opened so many doors for Rico and I knew that this was God's plan for Rico's new career path. What I couldn't anticipate was God's timing. Rico and I were both devastated when his application to UC Davis Medical School was denied. We cried out in anguish to God, not understanding why after all this time and work and prayer, Rico would be denied.

We learned a lot during that season. God had other work for us to do.

It was a devastating loss. Rico was crushed. He felt like he'd been doing everything God wanted him to do and doing it precisely. It was a defeating blow. I remember being incredibly disappointed for Rico but also for us. In our entire relationship, Rico had always wanted to be the provider in our family but I had usurped that position. I was ready for Rico to take over the leadership of our family and become the primary provider. Why would God stop him now?

We were so busy trying to get on track with our lives, we hardly noticed that this denial to medical school was also occurring during our most difficult marital struggle. What we didn't see was that it came at a time when Rico would not have been able to balance the demands of medical school and still have the energy and focus necessary to work on repairing our marriage. In hindsight we both agree, if Rico had been accepted into the PA program when he first applied, our marriage would certainly have failed.

Rico continued working at the head trauma clinic while we simultaneously steered hard into our broken relationship and God raised it from the dead. Literally. Once our marriage was on solid ground and Rico was able to reapply to PA school, he did so and was promptly accepted.

It taught us once again to 'trust God with all our heart and lean not on our own understanding' (Proverbs 3:5). God's perspective and omniscience are simply more than we can comprehend.

We had a family meeting, me, Rico and our boys and together we made a pact. We knew it wouldn't be easy. Dad would have to quit his job and fully immerse himself into two years of intense medical school. The boys and I would be essentially on our own. God had just recently blessed me with a full time position at Pacific Bell that promised to meet all our financial needs for the upcoming season.

The boys and I were excited for Rico and agreed to do everything we could to make it happen. We outlined details with things like adjusting the budget to dialing down the volume of the TV so Rico could study. We made a plan to save money each month so we could reward ourselves with a trip to Australia once he graduated.

For two full years we watched... when Rico wasn't in school, he would sit for hours on end at a small desk in the corner of our bedroom studying the world of medicine. It felt like boot camp. I know he thought he was drinking from a fire hose most of the time, but he never gave up. There were family camping trips during that time, and while the rest of us were sitting around a campfire Rico sat in the car with his medical books and a headlamp, studying. He was completely committed.

In the winter of 1999, Rico graduated from UC Davis Medical School and became a Physician Assistant. Ten months later we made good on the family pact and went to Australia. For three glorious weeks we visited extended family and experienced flora and fauna we'd never seen before in the most exquisite parts of Australia. We dove in the Great Barrier Reef, petted kangaroos and held koalas. It was a grand reward to launch Rico into his career as a health care provider.

As if completing medical school in his 40's wasn't enough, Rico went on to get a Master's degree in Medicine and is currently (in his 60's) completing a certificate in Functional Medicine. His commitment to keeping his craft sharp and up to date is more than admirable.

Rico is equally committed to keeping himself, and all those he cares about, healthy and vibrant. He works out regularly and enjoys challenging himself climbing 14,000 foot mountains with the men in the family and a multitude of friends.

Rico is now the leader he was always meant to be in our family. He is my partner in faith; we pray together about everything. We often pray throughout the day, at mealtimes and in the evening. We ask God to break our hearts for what breaks his, and he does. And it leads us to pray beyond our own circumstances.

Rico is my biggest cheerleader, but he is also brutally honest and gives me straight answers when I ask for them. He is my encourager and comforter and lifts me up when I'm down. He has learned to sit beside me and just hold me when I'm overwhelmed with one of those tidal waves of missing my son and grandchildren. He knows that I just need him to be there to grieve the loss with me and not to try to fix it for me.

Rico is thoughtful, supportive, kind and does sweet things for me to show me that he loves me and wants to lighten my load of responsibilities. Every time he does something like that, I marvel at how unworthy I am of his love and how blessed I am because of it.

He is an amazing father, husband, brother, son and friend. The world is a better place because Rico is in it. His capacity for love and forgiveness is matched only by his devotion to serving God. Rico humbly takes on leadership roles in our church. He is not satisfied with just getting by; he wants to serve God with everything he has, and I know there's no stopping him.

Over the course of our relationship, Rico and I have both grown a lot and amazingly, we've grown together. A trusted therapist once told us he had never seen two people more diametrically opposite in every way than the two of us. And yet, over time, we have become one. Our relationship has traversed the dark valleys of betrayal and lack of respect. With God firmly planted in the center of our life, we have made it to the other side. We have prevailed.

I am so grateful for "Rico", my Michael. The love of my life.

19

GRACE IN THE DARKNESS

Even though I walk with God constantly, I still have my ups and downs. Even knowing that the God of the Universe loves me and considers me his child does not make for a happily-ever-after world. It's more like being in the trenches with God. Just like everyone else, my heart gets heavy from time to time. But because I have devoted my heart to God he has assured me that he will always have my best interests in mind and will never, ever leave me. God enables me to cope with the difficult moments in life.

One of the best methods of working through grief is journaling. If I fall back into a pit of darkness, I grab my journal and begin writing to God. It's there where I pour out my feelings, crying out to God my innermost wishes and fears. I have come to believe that fear and worry are a mild form of atheism, but I believe my God is big enough to understand that I am still fragile. He knows what I'm thinking long before I say it out loud or scribe it in my journal, so I just cry out with honesty and then I wait for the Spirit to intercede on my behalf.

My journals also contain scribbled notes from dream frag-
ments that I quickly try to capture before being distracted by
the new day. In one of these, my dream was so vivid I can recall it nearly word perfect without even reviewing the journal.

"It was late at night, a dark and ominous feeling
surrounded me...rainy, misty...colored lights reflected off the wet streets. I am barefoot standing at a four-way intersection with cars zipping
all around me. My light was red and I watched
vehicles of all sizes scream across the intersection. I couldn't see beyond the ribbons of cars
because the road crested along the highway
and dipped down on the other side. I knew my
light was about to turn green so I got ready to
run. Fear kept me behind the line for a long
couple of seconds and then I ran for my life. It
was a lot harder than I expected and I feared
I wouldn't make it to the other side before the
light changed. I poured it on, running as fast
as I could. It took forever to reach the center
of the intersection where I could get a view of
the other side. What I found looked like the
remnants of a massive explosion. Enormous
blocks of concrete and asphalt were precari-
ously balanced in a giant random heap. I
quickly assessed the situation and kept running, leaping from one jagged chunk to another. I had to run fast but I couldn't see where
I was going. It was dangerous and frightening
but if I stopped or slowed down I would be hit

by oncoming traffic. I raced ahead and leapt forward, flying high toward the other side... and then I woke up."

When I look back on journal entries like the one above I can see God's hand at work. He was telling me that I am on a journey with choices. I could choose to get off the road and play it safe or I could choose to run for my life into the unknown where God IS. One of my all-time favorite verses of scripture is from Isaiah 42:16, which says, "I will lead the blind by ways they have not known. Along unfamiliar paths I will guide them. I will turn darkness into light before them and make the rough places smooth. These are the things I will do. I will not forsake them."

And so I continue running passionately on the path God has planned for me.

My journal is also the most effective tool I have for getting myself out of being stuck. I use my journal as a letter to God, usually starting with something like, "Good morning, God. Thank you for this day. Today I say, 'YES,' to whatever you have in store for me."

I try to start by counting my blessings but on some days I just need to ask why. Why am I separated from those I love? Why is my friend dying? Why do some people have to fight so hard for so long? It's been painful to write my story, because it required that I revisit my darkest hours, my most humiliating behaviors and openly confess my faults and weaknesses to my readers. More than once I've paused to wonder if I heard God correctly when he told me to, "Tell my story." But I know the answer. He didn't tell me once. It is woven through the last 15 years of journals...

Just the other day, I picked up my journal and wrote, "I'm tired, my heart is heavy, and I am filled with grief. I am tired of reviewing my life, reliving the darkness and shame all over again."

I continued journaling, "For months now I have been walking back through my history. It's felt like scavenging through a dark alley filled with garbage. Shining a bright flashlight I am bent over with this sharp stick, pulling back the disgusting bits of trash, investigating every corner." I emptied my heart to God. "I don't want to do this anymore. I am weary and I want to stop."

As I wrote, pouring out my emotion, God's Spirit inside me, interceded for me as He regularly does, and before I even finished emptying my plea, God started showing me His perspective.

"Maybe there's another way to look at it," I wrote.

I paused, put my pen down and took a deep breath. Then I picked up my pen and continued my dialogue. "I can choose to look back and see all the ugliness, OR with that same stick in the same dark alley, I can poke the same garbage, and instead of seeing my shame, I can find God's grace." I know it's there. It has to be or I wouldn't be here today writing this book.

It was a jolting thought. Suddenly I felt like I was in the midst of God's presence. Holy ground. I continued to write: "But that's a choice. To choose to see grace instead of the grief is a choice."

And then it hit me. Is this why God told me to write my story? Is this the reason for putting my story down on paper? "God, is this why I'm writing my story, so you can help me enter into an even deeper, more intimate relationship with you?"

Sitting there with my journal, I was overwhelmed with the feeling that God was so personally inviting me to step into those dark, ugly places of my history. But this time, I could see it from His perspective; to see what He did there. How He was there.

I wrote, "Wow. 'And we know that in all things God works for the good of those who love him, who have been called according to his purpose.' Romans 8:28 Once again you make the truth of Romans 8:28 come alive."

I continued to write, feeling closer to God with each stroke of my pen. "Once again you turn all things to good. My eyes are wet with tears as I see the grace. I am overcome with the realization that to enter into this place, means spending more time in those dark alleys. It means studying the situation so I can look more closely to find your grace. And there is so much to see." I said yes to the invitation.

I already knew what would happen, because I had been there before. I felt humbled deeply and gratitude flowed freely across my confused and happy face. Why was I so puzzled, that again, the God of the Universe was personal enough to care about me - to walk me through that? This was not a new sensation. I have regularly experienced this kind of intimacy with God through my journaling.

Now that I am looking through those sad, dark days of my life, through a new lens of God's grace, these are the blessings I've discovered.

Grace in Forgiveness

I am forever grateful and humbled by God's and Michael's forgiveness. I think about it often. It's become part of who I am, this layer of gratitude and humility. In Psalm 103:11-12, it says, "For as high as the heavens are above the earth, so great is his love for those who fear him; as far as the east is from the west, so far has he removed our transgressions from us." I know I have been forgiven by God and yet the knowledge of my past is always just beneath the surface. I think it's my way of ensuring I don't forget and make those same mistakes again. I am also in complete awe that my husband was willing to forgive me for betraying our marriage. Not only was he willing to stick it out, he worked hard with me to make it a great marriage! Even today, I'm still blown away by that.

Grace in Financial Stability

So much of my life was spent living in financial turmoil. Today, Michael and I enjoy being financially stable and it's such a blessing. I think about growing up where Mom would get a credit card in the mail, dad would be on a trip, and Mom considered the card free money. If she had checks in her checkbook, she pretended she had money in the bank. It was where I first learned about Retail Therapy. Mom went into debt to provide lavish gifts to people she barely knew. With that as my standard, I never learned financial responsibility. I fell into credit card debt, thinking that the money I expected to materialize in the next month would cover my spending today. As I look back, more maturely, I can see that I spent money I didn't have yet, three or four times before it arrived. A $500 commission check was coming and I'd spend it over and over again. And sadly, more often than I care to admit, that $500 check would never materialize. I was out of control when it came to finances.

Michael suggested we establish a budget and it felt like a father-daughter relationship had emerged instead of a partnership. I was the bad daughter who couldn't manage money, and Michael was the righteous father saying, "You're irresponsible financially and I'm going to sit you down and teach you how to do it right." That's how we started correcting my behavior, and I didn't like it at all. I had been the primary bread winner for most of my life and I felt entitled to spend money as I saw fit. Nevertheless, I had to admit there was a problem. And her name was Pamela.

Ultimately, I found huge freedom in turning my finances over to God. Once our budget had all the necessary elements, when it was expanded to include extra things we needed, it became freedom within discipline. God showed me clearly the means within which he expected me to live and I was more than content. We've been blessed with so much. I find it interesting how much I want to be on a budget now after I loathed it for so many years.

Trusting God with our finances is freeing because I have learned that he never lets us down. We always have what we need and we still give generously to others. My perspective on "stuff" has changed drastically over the years too. Not only am I more content and less likely to be tempted by shiny-things, instead of feeling 'entitled', I am humbled and grateful knowing we have so much.

The Grace of Restored Relationships

My story contains an assortment of painful, broken relationships, which through the grace of God have been restored.

Before my mother died, I was able to look back through my life and find empathy for that orphaned 14 year old who stopped growing emotionally. I forgave her and accepted her at the end of her life journey. I remember her now for the deep love she had for her grandchildren and her zest for life.

It was through grace that I was able to rekindle my relationship with my father. Shortly before Dad died, I was able to forgive him for leaving me and it renewed my love for him. And years after Dad died, Nora reached out to me. We talked about our past and settled into a place of forgiveness.

Writing my story also gave me the opportunity to sit down one-on-one with my sister for the first time in more than 10 years. It was the first time I learned the depth of what she experienced as a child. My heart was at once broken for what she endured and overjoyed at having a new level of intimacy with my precious sister. We grieved that we didn't have that conversation 50 years earlier and committed to remaining close the rest of our days.

My story also includes the rebuilding of a relationship with Husband #2, the father of my oldest son; a man who has become a good friend. Over the years Michael and I have become very close with H#2, his dear wife and precious daughter. They are our family. H#2 is an amazing man who went on to become a passionate professor of anthropology, sharing real life stories from his extensive experience working with the homeless population of Sacramento. I am proud of the man he is today and grateful for the ongoing relationship between us.

And of course, the most remarkable grace of all – the rebuilding of my marriage to Michael, which resulted in the most amazing love story.

The Grace of Other Mothers

Growing up with my mom, left me without many of the life lessons most little girls absorb through observation and role modeling. Nevertheless I have been blessed with many "other mothers;" most notably, my first mom-in-law, Jan, my last mom-in-law, Melba, and my spiritual mom, Marty. Each one, in their own way, gave me the gift I never knew I wanted. I was so busy growing up, trying to survive and take care of Mom, at the time I didn't know what I was missing. These women loved and nurtured me. They actively listened and offered advice if asked. They encouraged me and supported me with no strings attached. It was beautiful.

Some 20 years after I had walked out on H#1, I came across an old box in the attic with some of his adorable baby pictures. I knew they belonged with his current family so I looked up his brother's address and sent a package. I enclosed the baby pictures and a letter I had written to H#1, his mom, Jan, and his brother...it was long overdue. In those letters I accepted responsibility for disrupting their lives. I owned my immaturity and made a sincere effort to apologize. I didn't expect to hear from any of them, but I felt so much better just having confessed and apologized to this family that did not deserve what I gave them. Surprisingly, about a year later, Jan called me. We met for dinner and had a grace-filled meal together. Jan told me how much she appreciated me sending that letter. Healing and closure took place that day.

Melba passed away recently at the age of 91. I miss her dearly and yet I will always hold her close in my heart. We never lived in the same state, but I always looked forward to the times when she came to visit. I would have loved to spend more time with her. In our early days, she kept me in check when she thought I wasn't taking proper care of her son and I loved her candor and maturity. Over time, God knit our hearts together so they were practically inseparable.

We had a connection I'd never had before and I will always treasure it.

I still adore the times I get to spend with Marty. Our very first meeting took place on the steps outside the Church office. I was heartsick over a broken relationship and I desperately needed someone to talk to. Marty got tapped. She greeted me with her unmistakable smile and walked me outside. Sitting on those steps, she just listened. With tenderness and strength she guided me through my grief and helped me find ways to cope. Our heartstrings were knotted together that day in a bond that can't be broken.

I thoroughly enjoy meeting "older ladies" because I know they have a wealth of knowledge to share. I want to be a life-long learner, soaking up the wisdom others have gained over the decades of their lives. I am so grateful for the blessings I continue to find in these relationships.

Deciding to pay it forward, I have tried to pass that gift along by being a surrogate mom to some children of other mothers. While in most cases their own moms are quite wonderful, my surrogate daughters have adopted me as their own. I love to pour myself into other women...young and old. In the deepest places we are all connected and I sincerely believe we are better off together.

Grace of Sons and Daughters from Other Mothers

My love is deep, for my two sons. But I also enjoy the grace of adopted sons and daughters from other mothers. Some of the most treasured are young people I worked with in Africa. First there's Jessica, wise beyond her years, married in our backyard, she is sold out for God and following passionately after Him. And there's George and Marieke, who I met in

Kenya. They are like a son and daughter to me with our heart-strings tightly interwoven. We served together, ministering to the 'least of these' and I treasure each memory.

Then there is Anna, the Kenyan daughter Michael and I sponsor through Christ's Hope International. I have been privileged to spend time with her in her village and I look forward to being a part of her life for as long as possible. I am so blessed to remain connected to these beautiful masterpieces of God.

The Grace of Sisterhood

As I mentioned earlier, for the last decade I was estranged from my only biological sister. I thought I had been written out of her life forever which left a big black void in my heart. Today, I am thrilled to have her back in my life and look forward to making up for lost time.

Before reconnecting with Kathy I filled that dark hole with other sisters. God provided deep friendships with people like my dear friend Laura who inspired me to memorize scripture. We've traveled to Kenya together and shared many moments of joy and grief. I also love my neighbor and gym partner Cindy. Our frequent trips to the gym or walks along the American River have joined our hearts in the most intimate places. And then there's my friend Penni, who uses her gift of American Sign Language to almost magically translate songs of worship into an art form with her expressive hands and face. She lifts my soul. And my friend Theresa, with whom I have shared the challenges of fibromyalgia, the joy of making art and many common life experiences. And my soul-sister Carrie, even though I've only known her for a couple of years, God bound us together from day one. And

I can't forget my sisters-in-law. I have been blessed by being welcomed into Michael's family in so many ways and having sisters-in-law is an extra bonus.

There are many more women who inspire me and care for me and with whom I feel a special sisterhood. I wish I could name each one. The funny thing is, I had few true girlfriends until the last 10 years or so. I spent so much time competing in a man's world that I never felt as comfortable around women. I'm so grateful God put me in places where I could trust and grow close to these sisters.

Grace in the Blessings of Grandchildren

At the time I am writing this book I have two grandchildren that I haven't seen in more than three years. They are 8 and 10 years old and I love them dearly. Over the years God has given me seasons when I was able to spend quality time with them. We enjoyed weekly trips to the library for Story Time, after which we played on the playground and fed ducks at the McKinley Park pond. We had pretend conversations with busy squirrels and spent hours upon hours reading together. We grew a garden from seed and then reaped the rewards with daily harvests that became soup for dinner... my beautiful granddaughter standing on a step stool to reach the counter so she could help clean the vegetables. I love remembering my bright-eyed grandson sitting on my lap, facing me with his legs wrapped around my waist, his quiet smile and inquisitive expression as his fingers wove in and out through Grandma's silver and golden curls.

I am blessed with these and many more precious memories and they sustain me as I wait for the day I will be able to see them again. Meanwhile, God brought me to the nursery at my church to love on other people's babies. And then he gave us Savannah, our adopted granddaughter who fills our lives with so much love. Before she was ever conceived her mama asked us to be grandparents. Savannah just turned eight and we have been privileged to be a significant part of her everyday life. Sometimes Savannah will stare deeply into my eyes as if she is searching for ancient wisdom that might be hidden there. We laugh together and talk about everything. She loves art, music, math, science and dance - just like her grandma! She fills me to overflowing.

Grace in Serving

I first experienced grace in serving with my spiritual mom Marty. During one of my darkest years, Marty took me by the hand to go with her to visit the sick and dying. Instead of those visits being sad or depressing, Marty made them glorious. Always wearing a contagious smile, she would greet those we were visiting with the love of Jesus. Those were authentic times. No pretenses. Life was hard for the people we visited and yet we found encouragement in God's Word and in his faithfulness. During that dark period in my life, those were moments of bright light and much grace.

Some years later I had a similar experience serving in Kenya. I often say I found my heart in Kenya. I never even had a thought about going to Africa until my soul-sister Laura went there on a mission trip in 2009. The day she left I felt like I had missed the boat. I couldn't wait for her to come back and plan a trip that I could join her on. I learned so much going to Kenya. For starters, relationships took on a whole new meaning. To shift from the distractions of radio, TV and the internet to investing in the lives of others. Simply spending time together, listening and telling, laughing and crying, sharing adventures... There is such richness there. Or the realization that there is nothing that compares with coming alongside a person who's been thrown away by society to show them the sincere, tangible love of Jesus.

I also learned that many of us in America simply have TOO MUCH - we are spoiled and completely out of touch with the difference between needs and wants. We have no clue what a difference we could make in the life of another if we gave up just one of our extravagances. I say this as a constant reminder to myself. I am grateful that God reminds me of the people I love in Africa as I make every decision. Perhaps best of all, I have tangibly experienced the greater joy of giving over receiving.

Grace in Renewed Health

Through the grace of God, I have been healed from long periods of chronic illness. It has literally been the difference between life and death. When my health failed, in the worst of the Fibromyalgia days, it could take two hours just to get out of bed and ready for work. I had to manage my schedule around numerous naps just to restore my strength. I was an invalid, taking handfuls of pills that only seemed to make things worse as my body was overcome with toxicity. I was nearly worthless. God wanted me to have so much more, but he let me crash, because that's the only way I was able to stop the insanity of being Superwoman.

As God began to restore my health, he put practitioners in my path that understood my condition and treated me as a whole person. I am amazed and grateful that I am now fit and healthy. Even in retirement, I get up each morning around

6:30 a.m. and make green smoothies for Michael and myself. Filled with kale, blueberries, spinach, bananas, protein powder and other healthy stuff, they may not look pretty but they taste great and I know my body appreciates the wholesome nutrition. I love creating delicious and healthy meals and snacks that support our active lifestyle.

After breakfast, I meet my neighbor and we go to the gym. If we have a time constraint we get right to a cardio workout and then hit the weight training circuit. Otherwise, I am drawn to any form of exercise that involves moving my body with music. On Mondays and Wednesdays you can find us in kick-boxing, my favorite way to get a full body workout! On other days we enjoy the Latin American inspired Zumba classes, which provide a cardio-dance workout using music and choreographed steps for a fun fitness party atmosphere. The music can range from jazz to African beats to country, hip-hop and even pop. I love dancing and the artistry of moving to music invigorates my soul. It feels good to get my heart pounding and to feel the strength of my healthy body. I also value the importance of alternating my cardio workouts with strength, core and balance training through yoga and Pilates. I love the combination of grace and power I find in these classes. I feel powerful when I work out, grateful for the ability and confident I could handle myself in a dark alley if need be.

I was able to renew my health through great determination and strength that could only come from God and dedicated practitioners. I have been given a second chance at a healthy life. I grow more and more in the knowledge that my body is a temple of the Holy Spirit. I am so grateful for this gift and I choose to honor God by staying healthy, active and celebrating life. It truly is a gift of grace.

Grace in the Gifts of Art and Introspection

For me, art has a way of transporting me to another world. There is a curiosity in me that wonders about the artist, about the subject, about the meaning or just the feeling I get when looking at the art of others. Fine arts have always been important to me. But as my faith grew, so did my passion for the art world. Since my first elective in high school, photography has been woven into the very fabric of who I am. I love capturing one-of-a-kind moments, looking at the world from various angles, celebrating the delicate way light touches a subject. I enjoy experimenting in many forms of fine art such as painting, water color, printmaking and collage. My studio is filled with my projects and I'm often redirected by new ideas or techniques. I will always be a student of art and creativity.

I am learning more and more that our body, mind and spirit contains a wealth of ancient wisdom and knowledge. We have the capacity for so much more, but we often miss it because of all the extraneous noise in the world. Even though I have spent most of my life as an extrovert, I find myself more and more valuing the stillness of quiet reflection and the art that inevitably flows forth.

I've been blessed to meet some amazing women who offer online opportunities to connect and find our voices through words and art. Offerings like Resonant Graffiti, Liberated Lines, and Intuit & Inspire encourage me to slow down, step out into nature, listen to the promptings in my soul and participate in activities such as "art bombing" my community. It's fun, exhilarating and a little bit rebellious. I've been so inspired. Some women have made beautiful pieces of art and hung them in a public restroom (when no one was looking). Others have written words of encouragement on post-it notes and stuck them to packages of diapers and wipes, tucked away on shelves at Target or Walmart. An anonymous love note… just what a frazzled mom would need at the right moment. It's all about sharing our lives, loving ourselves and loving one another.

Another method of introspection I recall with gratitude is the sand-tray therapy I did with one of my dear therapists, Jozeffa, many years ago. Handing me a small basket she would direct me to her shelves full of everything miniature where I would collect a dozen or so items that I was attracted to. I would then position them in a large tray of sand and together we would unravel the meaning. In every case it was SO revealing.

I am an avid writer and I have kept a journal for decades. I am especially grateful for how God allows me to use my journal as a dialogue with him as well as a means to connect and re-integrate with parts of me I had locked away for many years. The grace of writing and the insight it offers is truly a divine blessing.

The Gifts and Grace of New Opportunities

I am now retired, but I am NOT done. I wrote this book because God told me to do so. I also felt God tell me that he would one day put me back into the world of public speaking.

What does that mean? Simply that I trust God will draw me to places where he has work for me to do. I have spoken to many groups and been well received over the years through my work with Dale Carnegie, as a Christian retreat leader, a keynote speaker, and even a guest host on a real estate radio talk show. I believe that God will put me in front of groups of people who need to be encouraged. My audience will hold people who've had life challenges, similar to mine, and can take heart in my victories. I trust God will use my stories to help others explore theirs. There are so many pieces that will connect: broken relationships, ruined finances, career challenges, health crises. I'm excited to see where God directs me to make those connections with people who can benefit from my encouragement. I am evidence that there's joy on the other side of the pain.

As I look back at my dark history through God's lens, I am astounded at the blessings I find in the garbage, and I've only scratched the surface. The depth of God's love is manifested in the thousands of ways he has turned everything in my life for good. He gives me hope in my grief. Revisiting my past is no longer as painful, my scars are evidence of God's grace. The wounds are healed and the lessons are poignant. They keep me on the path of faithfulness. God is in charge today. Superwoman has left the building.

20

WISDOM OF THE AGES

One of my greatest lifetime take-a-ways is the understanding that we are all valuable... just the way we are. What we do or how well we do it isn't the point. We are each a hand-crafted one-of-a-kind masterpiece of the Creator of the Universe. You, are a priceless work of art and he loves you more than you can imagine. He made a plan for you before the beginning of time...'a plan to prosper you and not to harm you; a plan to give you hope and a future' (Jeremiah 29:11). He wants SO much for you.

From my perspective, it is nothing short of a miracle that I finally came to the place where I was ready to give God a shot.

Once I set aside my preconceived notions and began to search out God's character, I found an intimate relationship I never expected. As I let His words soak deeply into my soul, I found comfort in his letters of love and words of encouragement. I know for some it might not feel like this is a right fit for you...this Jesus. And I totally respect that. I can only speak for myself. Having thoroughly tried atheism and looked into other types of faith, pure faith in Jesus as the Risen Son of

God is just the only thing that makes sense to me. I can't fully explain it, but I know it is real.

Once I fully committed my life and my marriage to God, things dramatically improved in my life. God always kept His promise, showing me steady progress in our marriage, and I kept my end of the deal by being fully committed to making it work. For so many years I had been looking for a Prince to take care of me and instead I found a King to serve.

I am amazed and humbled and incredibly grateful that our God is so patient. My husband and I have now been married more than 32 years and my love for him continues to grow every day. I have no desire to be with anyone else.

One of the greatest blessings from all of this is the example we've provided for our sons. While they did not know all the sordid details of my past until I committed this to paper, they knew things changed for the better many years ago. They have watched me and Michael work together and resolve conflict with respect and kindness. Trevor still laughs and shakes his head as he watches us approach an issue from opposite sides of the fence. Nevertheless, he would have to agree, we always end up on one side, together. Our sons have observed that we are deeply committed to our faith and our family, and they have seen that we are unwavering in those commitments.

I took the long and winding road for many years before I accepted Christ, and even then, I did it half-heartedly. Still, God took my feeble step and showed me his love over and over again. I had to get to the place where I realized that if God could forgive me and accept me, in spite of all the times I had effectively spit in his face, then I needed to do whatever I could to honor him and love him in return.

So…what does the bible say God wants from us? It's pretty simple.

Love Him and love others. Forgive others as he forgave us.

When you put us up against his benchmark of love and forgiveness, there is just no comparison. We could never love and forgive others anywhere near as much as God loves and forgives us. But I believe those are my marching orders and that is what I try to do. I start every day knowing that I long to please the God who made me and loves me beyond my wildest imagination. I start each day looking freshly upon the people I meet. I try to look at others through God's eyes, knowing, no matter what, he made them and wants me to love them. I am his ambassador, Jesus with skin on. God counts on those of us who have accepted his free gift of grace to be his hands, feet, arms and mouth to those around us.

That is why I see people differently now. I rarely judge others harshly because I know that if I were judged as I deserve I would be writhing in a pit somewhere. Believe me, this has been a process. It didn't happen overnight. When I am faced with painful experiences and crushing betrayals, all I can do is draw close to God, and he gives me his assurance that he will carry my burden. My part, is to stop judging and keep loving. And it is working. I will never stop loving others, because God will never stop loving me.

This does not mean we are Christian doormats, laid out for anyone who pleases to walk on whenever they want. It does not mean we are to take abuse or that we must be reconciled with those who have caused us pain. But it does mean we are to forgive them and let God handle the details. Staying in the game may mean that I am vulnerable to getting hurt again. But I am willing to take that risk, knowing that God will hold me close no matter what happens.

As I look back over my life I appreciate the bits of wisdom I have gleaned through the shards of my broken past...

My life story is a clear example of how we really don't know what is going on in the lives, hearts and minds of those around us. When interacting with those around me, I try to assume the best of them.

If I were to ask the dozens of people I see and serve at church each week (who haven't heard my story), I would bet my retirement they would say I am all put together and was born that way. But that's not the truth.

So when I see other people acting out or behaving strangely or making bad choices, instead of judging, I wonder. What's going on in that person's life that would cause them to do such a thing? Inevitably there is deep pain or unresolved conflict buried inside. So what do we do? LOVE them. Offer a SMILE... or a KIND word. You might just be the first person who has done that in a very long time.

I've also learned a lot about "owning my own stuff" and not projecting it on others. If I am faced with a conflict or a challenging relationship I no longer automatically point blame at those around me. I'm not saying everything is always my fault, but I am saying that the only thing I can control is my part. So I ask God to show me what he would have me learn in each and every circumstance. When I am honest and vulnerable with God, he gently shows me how to be in that situation. He reminds me of verses I have memorized like Psalm 46:10, which says, "Be still and know that I am God." Or Exodus 14:14, which says, "The Lord will fight for you, you need only be still."

I also have to ask myself if this is a recurring pattern. We are so amazingly capable of deceiving ourselves... I am still blown away that it took three divorces and nearly losing my fourth marriage before I realized that I was the common denominator. I had to look hard through my past to identify the driving forces that kept propelling me to try and find love in all the wrong places.

Another big lesson for me has been embracing my emotions. Some of us are taught to suck it up...don't cry...be tough! Others, like myself, observe the frightening display of emotions like anger and we swear we will never behave like that. So we lock up our anger...and sometimes people think we don't care. This is a huge topic and I am so grateful for the opportunities I've had to get in touch with the repressed parts of who I am. We were created with immense emotion. We are made to love and laugh and cry and hurt and grieve and start all over again. And we are made to do it together...

I've learned that when I don't embrace my emotions...when I try to ignore the angst in my soul...it will always find a way out. Pay now or pay later. As a Geography major living in California I am sensitive to the active and dormant volcanoes in our region. For years I lived like a volcano, stuffing pain and other feelings I didn't know what to do with deep down inside. Like molten lava it boiled and churned. Periodically throughout the years a small fissure would erupt, releasing a bit of the pressure, and I would experience paralysis from the waist down... or a case of spinal meningitis or trigeminal neuralgia...or a case of shingles. The more I kept stuffing, the greater the power built, until finally the entire top of my mountain blew right off. And I was exposed... I learned you can't put it back once it has exploded. Now, as painful as it is sometimes, I want to feel everything. All the highs, all the lows and everything in between...and I am so much richer and wiser because of it.

While writing this book I have looked back and I can see signs of who I was and who I was meant to be... but I lacked confidence. I was afraid to just be me. Afraid I wasn't enough. So I became a student of human behavior without even realizing it. I would observe my environment, determine what I needed to do to be accepted and feel safe in that environment, and that is who I became. I was a chameleon. It wasn't until I had secured the deal and safely landed a husband that I would start to let the real me out... It's no wonder I felt so much judgement.

If I had it to do over again I would want people in my life that encouraged me to be ME. I wouldn't have rushed into marriage but instead I would have rushed into therapy. I would have spent more time exploring what was important to me...my values, my dreams, my passions, my gifts and my talents. I would have embraced God and accepted His partnership in my life much sooner. I truly believe God created each one of us personally. He made us with special gifts and talents that He intended us to use for the benefit of all of His creation. Even the things that others might find quirky God designed to be unique and special about us. If I had it to do over again I would EMBRACE all that I am, complete with flaws and failures, and I would try hard not to miss a thing.

The older I get the more aware I am that our world is full of hurting people. God has broken my heart for what breaks his and I just want us to LOVE one another... reach out... practice random acts of kindness. I love remembering how we taught our boys that whenever possible, as we crossed a toll bridge we would prepay for the car behind us, regardless of whether we knew them. It was always amusing to see the car pass us with the driver's window rolled down, money in hand with a confused look on their face. They never quite understood. Then one day when Trevor, as a young driver, was coming back from the coast with some buddies, he accidentally got on the wrong road and ended up in San Francisco. To get out he had to cross a toll bridge but he had no money. As he pulled up to the toll booth to explain the situation the attendant just waived him on telling him the car ahead had already paid. He couldn't believe it. First hand he experienced the receiving end of a random act of kindness. He couldn't wait to share that story with us and now we all continue the practice.

There are so many ways we can love one another. It can be as simple as looking into the eyes of a stranger while offering a warm, sincere smile. Or taking the time to send a handwritten note of encouragement... There are countless ways we can demonstrate love and kindness. We just need to decide to DO IT.

It can be a little bit scary, but if you're willing, ask God to direct you to people he wants you to meet. I have been blessed time and again when I open myself up to others. Notice the children. Be an encourager! Build others up! And when words fall short in the impossibly hard times...come alongside, and just BE with one another. Sometimes that is the best way you can love.

Spread love...thick like peanut butter. And as you are spreading love, remember to begin with loving yourself. As they say on all commercial flights, "You must first attend to your own mask before assisting others with theirs..."

For many of us we've been wearing masks for decades, hiding behind the pain and shame, the bitterness and grief. We've put on our most acceptable face every day and we've put one foot in front of the other. We have survived. But God wants us to THRIVE.

When I think of what it was like before I finally surrendered completely to God, it was like walking through life with a heavy-ply translucent veil draped over me. I could still function, but it was constricting and I couldn't see clearly. Everything was hazy. And now, each day that I start with God, I see LIFE. It's a daily choice but when I consciously look, I see it everywhere... From the vibrant crimson leaves of the Japanese Maple just before they drop for winter, to the little girl with sparkling diamonds for eyes at the table next to mine at Panera's... From the one-legged man who cleans windshields while I shop, to the horses in the pasture just up the street from us... I even see it in the dust bunnies that pop up in the sunshine as it crosses my hard wood floors in the mornings – and I stop – and think of the millions who live without a home...without hard wood floors on which to collect dust bunnies. I stop to remember that they are each masterpieces of God and I lift them in prayer. Our spirits are connected and we are one. It is a FULL life.

Don't get me wrong, I'm not always that tuned in. But I try to be. I want to be. Because I know what it's like. It is a FULL life and I am grateful.

If any of this is resonating with you, please know you are not alone. It is so hard to ask for help... It never even occurred to me for much of my life. Yet I am convinced that God designed us to be interdependent rather than independent. He designed us each with different gifts and abilities so that together we can come alongside one another and provide what we can't accomplish by ourselves.

Sometimes help comes in the form of a friend or relative that you can trust. Other times it may be a therapist you feel comfortable with or a safe support group like Celebrate Recovery. Some of my greatest healing has happened in the midst of a small group of friends...people I could trust while I learned about God's promises and desires for me. The healing happened because we met regularly and held each other accountable. By being honest and vulnerable, we allowed real transformation to take place.

In the words of a favorite prayer recorded in the Bible, "I pray that you, being rooted and established in love, [18] may have power, together with all the saints, to grasp how wide and long and high and deep is the love of Christ, [19] and to know this love that surpasses knowledge – that you may be filled to the measure of all the fullness of God." Ephesians 3:17-19

More than anything in the world, I pray that if you are reading this book, you will give God a chance to love you like you have never been loved before. Give him a chance to accept you, flaws and all. Give him a chance to redeem the mistakes you have made. He can turn them into blessings. I pray that you might give God a chance to be everything to you.

All you have to do is invite him into your life. His arms are open, his hands are reaching out to you. It's a simple prayer, you can recite out loud or in your heart, with these words, or your own:

"Jesus, please forgive me for all the ways I've failed. I believe in my heart that your death on the cross has paid for my sins. I want a relationship with the God who made me and I thank you for your unconditional love, and for the gift of eternal life. Please give me wisdom, strength and courage to walk in your will. Amen."

It is such a relief knowing I don't have to have all the answers. Letting go of expectations is also a relief…. I know people will fail me and I know I will fail others. But I also know that God will never turn away from me. He loves me and he loves you and He will always be with us in every situation…

Be blessed.
Pamela

> "So let's do it—full of belief, confident that we're presentable inside and out. Let's keep a firm grip on the promises that keep us going. He always keeps his word. Let's see how inventive we can be in encouraging love and helping out, not avoiding worshiping together as some do but spurring each other on, especially as we see the big Day approaching." Hebrews 10:21-25 - Message

ABOUT THE AUTHOR

 Pamela McClanahan lives in Northern California, with her husband Michael and her dog Frida. She is all about relationships! Active in Church, she loves spending time with her family and friends. Pamela loves animals and nature and is rarely seen without her camera. In her spare time, you'll find her creating art in her studio, much of which is inspired by the mission work she has done primarily in Kenya. An avid writer and blogger, Pamela balances her computer time with Kickboxing and Zumba classes.

A warm and passionate communicator, Pamela is available as a keynote speaker or retreat leader. You can find her at www.pamelamcclanahan.com or email her directly at pamelamcclanahan4@gmail.com.

Made in the USA
San Bernardino, CA
19 April 2017